'Outside of religious institutions there has not been much published guidance on how to create rituals. Beginning in the mid-20th century though, wedding planners, along with celebrant, humanist and funeral societies, began to fill the void. Half a century later, DIY rituals can still be awkward, embarrassing or meaningless. This book takes a decisive step in the right direction. It gives practical advice to readers for crafting rites of passage thoughtfully and creatively.'

> – *Ronald L. Grimes, author of* The Craft of Ritual Studies *and professor emeritus in the Department of Religion and Culture at Wilfrid Laurier University in Waterloo, Ontario, Canada, ronaldlgrimes.twohornedbull.ca*

'*Crafting Secular Ritual* draws on Jeltje Gordon-Lennox's wealth of experience and her gentle, compassionate nature. This practical handbook will be enormously helpful to all those interested in carving out unique, meaningful, relevant and profound secular rituals for life events of all kinds.'

> – *Lindy Mechefske, journalist and author of* Sir John's Table *and* A Taste of Wintergreen, *Kingston, Ontario, Canada, lindymechefske.com*

'A fascinating and erudite work on a rich subject that manages to bridge the practical and the theoretical, the broad brush stroke and the minutest detail, in a way that is enjoyable to read and easy to understand. As an independent celebrant, I found it both informative and inspiring, filled with ideas that cover a breadth of rituals that our secular society so clearly needs. Whether you are a professional maker of ritual, wishing to deepen the understanding of how and why human beings ritualize their experiences, or an individual driven by an interest in creating secular ritual to help cross a life threshold, this book will provide the reader with a rich foundation for the creation of meaningful experiences.'

> – *Tiu de Haan, celebrant, facilitator and speaker, London, UK, http://tiudehaan.com*

'We have forgotten how to make rituals; the lack of ritual in our lives today leads to alienation and loneliness. By neglecting ritual we lose out on an aspect of life that human beings once gave their utmost attention. This book appeals to all, secular and religious. It allows us to reconsider one of the greatest human needs: our ritual life.'

> – *Gianpiero Vincenzo, author of* New Ritual Society: Consumerism and Culture in Contemporary Society *and sociologist at the Fine Art Academy of Catania, Sicily, Italy*

'The time has certainly come for a book like this, which carefully, thoroughly and skilfully describes why ritual is important, how ritual can be created and realized in secular society with people who are either distanced from their root religious traditions, or who have a secular mind set, or little meaningful relationship with any traditional religion. This book contains helpful graphs, lists and directions for creating ritual, and describes the role and duties of presiders or celebrants of secular ritual. This is a handbook and reference book which can be used in many ways in a huge variety of circumstances, and I personally want very much to have it in my library. It is rich with scholarship, careful thought, clear explanations and inspired wisdom.'

– The Reverend Marchiene Rienstra, interfaith
and unity minister, Sedona, Arizona

'This book addresses all aspects of contemporary ritualmaking. The author speaks to her reader's heart and mind. The language is clear and concrete. This book is interesting for scholars, celebrants and everyone looking for ways to meaningfully ritualize life-transitions.'

– Joanna Wojtkowiak, PhD, cultural psychologist and assistant
professor, University of Humanistic Studies, The Netherlands

'*Crafting Secular Ritual* is perfectly written to meet the need of contemporary people for meaningful ritual in their lives without necessarily turning to religious traditions that may not resonate with them or their loved ones. Jeltje Gordon-Lennox provides a blending of historical context with modern tools and checklists that provides the scaffolding needed for those who will create rituals for themselves or on behalf of others. As a Unitarian Universalist minister, I often create personalized rituals for a wide range of people who are religious, spiritual and/or completely secular. This new addition to the body of work supporting the need for ritual to mark major life passages and events combined with a detailed methodology for crafting these rituals is most welcome.'

– Reverend Margaret A. Beckman, pastor at the Unitarian
Universalist Congregation of Castine, Maine

CRAFTING

SECULAR

RITUAL

A PRACTICAL GUIDE

Jeltie Gordon - Lennox

Foreword by Isabel Russo

Jessica Kingsley *Publishers*
London and Philadelphia

Identity icon by © Adaiyaalam CC BY-SA
All other figures and icons © J. Gordon-Lennox
Photos © Ida van der Lee

First published in 2017
by Jessica Kingsley Publishers
73 Collier Street
London N1 9BE, UK
and
400 Market Street, Suite 400
Philadelphia, PA 19106, USA

www.jkp.com

Copyright © Jeltje Gordon-Lennox 2017
Foreword copyright © Isabel Russo 2017
Author photo copyright © Graham Haber

Front cover image source: Sophie Standing.

Library of Congress Cataloging in Publication Data
Names: Gordon-Lennox, Jeltje, author.
Title: Crafting secular ritual : a practical guide / Jeltje Gordon-Lennox.
Description: London ; Philadelphia : Jessica Kingsley Publishers, [2017] |
    Includes bibliographical references and index.
Identifiers: LCCN 2016022346 | ISBN 9781785920882 (alk. paper)
Subjects: LCSH: Rites and ceremonies. | Ritual. | Secularism.
Classification: LCC GT95 .G65 2017 | DDC 203/.8--dc23

British Library Cataloguing in Publication Data
A CIP catalogue record for this book is available from the British Library

ISBN 978 1 78592 088 2
eISBN 978 1 78450 350 5

Printed and bound in Great Britain

MIX
Paper from
responsible sources
FSC
www.fsc.org   FSC® C013056

For my children Sushila and Jefferson

CONTENTS

Ritual Toolbox: List of Tools with Their Icons   8

Foreword by Isabel Russo   11

Acknowledgements   14

Preface   16

PART I · OUR RITUAL HERITAGE   21

1. From Rock Art to Ritual Art   22
2. The Sense of Ritual   31

PART II · RITUAL THROUGH CRAFT   41

3. Guidelines for Ritualizing   42
4. Ritual Materials and Design   50
5. A Ritual Toolbox   63

PART III · CRAFTING MEANINGFUL RITUAL   91

6. Birth and Beginnings   93
7. Coming of Age   107
8. Marriage   117
9. Growing Up, Growing Old   131
10. Death and Endings   139
11. Ritualizing in Public Spaces   153

Conclusion   163

References   165

Index   170

RITUAL TOOLBOX
LIST OF TOOLS WITH THEIR ICONS

CHECKLIST

PLANNING PHASE

Questionnaire on ritual identity

Key to Questionnaire on ritual identity

Five techniques for feeling safe

Hugging (Using touch with others)

Butterfly hug (Using touch alone)

Near and far (Eyes)

Humming (Voice and breath)

Heavenly drum (Ears)

Prioritizing

Who presides?

CREATING PHASE

Why and how?

Core values

Plumbing the meaning of core values

Mapping it out

Coherence test

Just the right music

Small gestures, big impact

Format of the ceremony

REALIZING PHASE

Ritualizing step by step

Guidelines for readers

Preparing your funeral

FOREWORD

The need for ritual is innate. We need ritual to enable us to connect with our deepest thoughts and feelings, our nascent hopes and our debilitating fears. We need it to re-connect us to our changing bodies and to our changing relationships, to help us create a language that authentically articulates our experience of ourselves in the world, and to speak that language both to ourselves and to those closest to us. We need ritual to create the technicolour signposts on our self-crafted map, signalling where we have come from and where we are going.

In an increasingly frantic world, ritual gives us punctuation. It gives us an essential pause that says:

Hey. Stop for a moment. Breathe. This really matters.

Removing god from the heart of a ceremony, be it a funeral, a wedding or a naming, can still feel to many like a radical, bold and unchartered step. It creates a profoundly significant shift of focus and of purpose, as in each case the person who has died, the couple who are getting married, the baby who has been born, are put at the centre, at the heart of the ritualizing. At the same time the community of family and friends are invested with the responsibility of 'bearing witness', humanizing instead of, as was previously the case, deifying the experience. Crafting secular ritual is an intimate, challenging and profoundly rewarding act of creation.

The British Humanist Association (BHA) has been conducting non-religious ceremonies since 1896, but it has seen demand grow exponentially in the last decade as people have become more aware of the secular option and increasingly emboldened to make a choice that genuinely reflects their own belief system. More and more people who choose to live their life without religion are allowing themselves to embark on a genuine and sincerely felt journey of what ceremony really means to them, rather than acquiescing to the charade of what it should mean.

Over the last eight years, both as a humanist celebrant and in my role as Head of Ceremonies at the BHA, responsible for a network of over 300 celebrants, I have been involved in the development of non-religious ritual in Britain. This has given me a strong sense of the emerging secular rituals that I hope one day will be viewed as an acceptable and integral part of life, as our non-religious naming, wedding and funeral ceremonies are finally becoming.

I first met Jeltje Gordon-Lennox at a Celebrant Trainers' Symposium in Utrecht at a time when I was tired and raw from an unexpected loss in my personal life. Over the next two days we discussed and developed thoughts on the key elements of successful celebrant training and the essential components of ritual. With her encouragement, we also designed the first draft of a powerful and deeply personal 'Death of a Marriage' ceremony, which I carried out on my own four months later, at a place and a time that had heart and meaning to me.

From my own experience of ritual, as a participant as well as a celebrant creating it and conducting it, I share Jeltje's perspective that ritual is born of a deep need to articulate times of profound experience and transition, and that it is an essential part of what makes – and keeps – us human. Like Jeltje, I also firmly believe that meaningful ritual – that is, ritual that reflects the subject's belief system and the core elements that have meaning for them – makes for a psychologically healthier individual and by extension, for a substantially healthier society. I have heard innumerable accounts from people who attended 'traditional' religious funerals that left them alienated, frustrated and depressed because the platitudes offered were at best, irrelevant and at worst, an offensive contradiction to the values held by the person who had died. The complex process of recognition, acknowledgement and letting go of the deceased cannot take place at this type of funeral, and so the grieving process and subsequent healing process are stymied.

In writing this outstanding guide, Jeltje Gordon-Lennox not only states a watertight case for the significance of secular ritual, but also more importantly provides us with a set of finely honed crafting tools and a clarion clear explanation of how to use them. She thereby charges us with the ability to carve for ourselves our very own profound and contemporary rituals, whoever we are, and wherever we are.

While Jeltje's voice is that of a highly skilled artisan, her academic's eye works alongside her practitioner's heart to deliver a comprehensive and compassionate toolbox with historical, biological, psychological and even neurological context. As we read, a powerful apprenticeship takes place and we are generously provided with excavating, creating and planning tools for each of the major birth, marriage and death rituals.

In addition, we are equipped with case studies and suggestions for the new rituals that are emerging, be they civic or deeply private, as taboos are addressed and the need for newly articulated signposts is uncovered.

Jeltje's extensive work as a psychotherapist, together with the 35 years she has spent presiding over both religious and secular rituals, and her keen knowledge of world religions and of ritual history, mean that she is able to bring a uniquely broad canvas of experience and perspective to this work.

Crafting Secular Ritual is a landmark book. I am delighted to be a part of this fascinating and necessary conversation, and even more delighted that, with this book, so many more people will be enabled to actively participate in the life-altering and life-affirming creation of meaningful ritual.

Isabel Russo
Head of Ceremonies, British Humanist Association
London, May 2016

ACKNOWLEDGEMENTS

Getting permission can be tough. When it comes to the really important things in life, there is often no one to ask: being born, dying, being happy... I did not ask for permission to do secular ceremonies. I am grateful to all those – in particular my family – who trusted me to help them make their life events special and to the celebrants who trained with me. This handbook is wrought of what you taught me.

Numerous friends and colleagues read all or part of this manuscript or contributed in other significant ways. Thank you all for your time and wisdom: Andrés Allemand Smaller, Sara Armstrong, Anastasia Aukeman, Franziska Bangerter Lindt, Margaret Beckmann, Christine Behrend, Isabelle Bourgeois, Siméon Brandner, Sara Rose Carswell, Douglas Fowley, Jr, Yuliya Grinberg, Eileen English Kaarsemaker, Fred Kaarsemaker, Isabelle Kostecki, Sharon Miller, Sharon Pettle, Lut Schops, Matthieu Smyth and Pierre Pradervand.

At one point, a reader asked: How *is* ritual devised? The audacity and scope of this project hit me square on. I came to ritual theory through a back door, as a practitioner, motivated by the needs of people around me for secular life event ceremonies. Matthieu Smyth kept me on track by piquing my curiosity and encouraging me to look at the role of the senses in ritualizing. Ronald L. Grimes's criticism and generous suggestions proved invaluable. Joanna Wojtkowiak's timely invitation to the Symposium for celebrant trainers in Utrecht opened several doors and put me in contact with key people. I was challenged to assume my model of ritualmaking as craft by Ellen Dissanayake's daring exploration of the origins of play, art and ritual. Robert Scaer's work and life inspire me. His quiet patience and optimism reassured me on more than one occasion. A special thank you to Natalie Watson at Jessica Kingsley Publishers for entrusting me with this project. Her encouragement and enthusiasm supported me throughout the writing process.

I am also deeply indebted to my production editor Alexandra Holmes, editorial assistant Hannah Snetsinger and marketing and publicity executive Lily Bowden for their expert advice, patience and close attention to the myriad of details that turn a manuscript into a book.

Above all, I want to acknowledge the support of Ian, my partner in life and companion in creativity. Our children, Sushila and Jefferson, inspired my work in this field. They and the challenges they face – often with laughter and equanimity – taught me that our human need to feel safe is an essential condition for bonding, cohesiveness and commitment to a common cause. As was the case for the early hunter-gatherer tribes, our survival, and that of our planet, depend on our capacity to make this happen today.

PREFACE

My first non-religious wedding ceremony was created for my sister and her husband in 2000. The couple upped the ante by combining it with a naming ceremony for their newborn daughter and honouring their Jewish and Christian cultures. I was flattered by their request and stimulated by the challenge. Nonetheless, I saw it as a one-off event: this kind of wedding was for trendy New Yorkers; it was unheard of in Europe. As we prepared their ceremony, I realized that – trendy or not – this was exactly what I was being asked to do in my parish in Switzerland. The situation put me wise to a major paradigm shift[1] in contemporary society. I stood on one side with the respectable clergy of religious institutions who proposed traditional rites; on the other were growing lines of people who wanted to celebrate the transitions of their lives without these religious trappings.

In the parish, I prepared funerals for atheist grandmothers whose family cried: 'We have to do something! She wasn't a dog!' I did weddings for young couples wanting 'a nice ceremony' with no references to god or religion, and baptisms for children who would never again cross the threshold of a church. Touched by these people's unmet needs for fitting ceremony, I spent a year preparing, and then resigned from my job. This decision marked the beginning of an intense period. For more than ten years I kept my head down – literally and figuratively – as I put an untried professional activity into place while caring for our young children and following my husband's music career. There was little time to wonder about what others were doing elsewhere, let alone muck about with theory.

Early on, a British couple working in Geneva contacted me to do their wedding ceremony. They explained that although they would not have

---

1   Scientist Thomas Kuhn popularized the concept of 'paradigm shift' over 50 years ago, arguing that scientific advancement is not evolutionary, but a 'series of peaceful interludes punctuated by intellectually violent revolutions'. During these revolutions 'one conceptual world view is replaced by another' (1996 [1962], p.10).

minded a church wedding, they did not want to offend religious friends who knew full well that the couple were not practising Christians. Shortly after that, a couple from Colorado called, asking me to help them with their wedding ceremony in Paris. This was a second marriage for both of them. As they moved into their late thirties, they observed that their needs had changed. They were less interested in tradition than in a ceremony that authentically marked their mature relationship and commitment. A recent death in the family made it a poor time for a big celebration, so their friends and family organized small receptions for them in four different states. Thanks to the internet, we crafted a ceremony that suited their need for intimacy and adventure in a quiet corner of a public park. After a champagne toast, the photographer and I accompanied the couple to the most famous sites in Paris for their wedding shoot. The newly-weds were applauded at each stop by busloads of tourists and Parisian well-wishers. Yet another couple who got engaged on a pier rented a holiday home near that spot so they could have a wedding ceremony on the lawn overlooking the lake. A group of buskers who impressed them was hired to play for the bride's arrival in a motorboat driven by her father. Two years later, they asked me to craft a naming ceremony for their daughter.

While I enjoy the challenges of wedding and naming ceremonies, I feel truly useful when I do funerals. From the first, I was called in to accompany people who lost loved ones under the most trying of circumstances: murder, suicide and the sudden death of a child. As with weddings, the ceremony is only the visible tip of the iceberg. The important work of accompaniment goes on behind the scenes. On top of the loss, tiny fissures in family relationships may burst open in an untimely manner with the volatile pressure of sorrow and old, unattended grief. Time and tempers are often short. Putting together a funeral outside traditional religious structures is a real challenge. A meaningful funeral ceremony faithfully reflects the deceased's values, life and relationships. In the first days after a death, few mourners feel ready to put words to their relationship with their loved one. Our culture is not geared to letting people emerge at their own rate from the shock of death and loss. Too often the bereaved feel pushed into making decisions designed to 'get the funeral out of the way' so that they can 'move on'. Even when a death is expected, mourners may need days or even a week or two to feel ready to work together on the funeral ceremony. When the bereaved can take the time they need to craft a fitting ceremony, they usually find the process of expressing their joy and sadness in a ceremonial setting remarkably healing.

As I accompanied people through their lifecycle events in non-religious settings, I realized that my own ritual identity had changed. Ritual studies scholar Catherine Bell's description of what happened to her resembles my experience:

> Once I was a believer, thoughtfully and intimately committed, and then I was no longer one, with a different set of thoughts and emotions. While I was able to 'explain' my believing and my not-believing in the popular Freudian patois of the day, I wanted to assemble a fuller picture of what had happened and explore whether what was true for me might be useful for understanding others. (Bell no date)

While Bell wanted to know what had happened, I wanted to know what comes next and to explore whether what was true for me might be useful for others. Could I help others meet their need for non-religious ceremony? Instinctively, I moved towards using creativity and rigour to craft new ceremonies, and included the senses as an important part of the equation. At the request of a local publisher I wrote two manuals – in French. When my second book came out, Matthieu Smyth, Professor of Ritual Anthropology at the University of Strasbourg (France), contacted me to talk about my practical approach. Our dialogue – now in its fifth year – brought me out of isolation. I eagerly discovered fresh vocabulary such as 'emerging ritual', and explored the myriad of fields in 'ritual studies', from psychology to art, performance and neuroscience, but I searched in vain for a practical take on the paradigm shift to *secular* ritualization.

> Ritual practice is the rhyme and rhythm of society.
>
> *David L. Hall and Roger T. Ames (1998, p.270)*[2]

My approach to the craft of secular ritual is based on more than 30 years of professional ritual practice in leadership roles within established religious institutions in North America and Europe, and enhanced by my role as an independent psychotherapist, secular celebrant and trainer. My model is influenced by my unique personal, linguistic and geographical vantage points. It is my hope that what works for me, my clients and the celebrants I have trained will be of use to others as they ritualize their life events.

This guide is intended as a simple hands-on approach to crafting secular ritual. It keeps the ritualmaker on course by concentrating on the essentials: Who or what is at the centre of this ceremony? What values do I want to convey? How can I transmit them simply and authentically? It should be adapted as needed to specific situations and contexts. Those who want recipes for ready-made ceremonies must look elsewhere. 'Ritual is work, endless work. But, it is among the most important things that we humans do' (Seligman *et al.* 2008, p.182).

If you are eager to get to work on a specific occasion, feel free to skip the more theoretical chapters in Part I. Part II is the heart of this handbook: it contains the guidelines to ritual design and materials as well as a practical toolbox that includes checklists to keep ritualmakers on course and free them up to fully experience the process and the ceremony. Part III applies these basic principles and tools to the ritualization of five transitions in life and public events.

---

2   The context for this quote is a discussion about ritual in Chinese thought: 'Ritual practices, then are "performances", social roles and practices that, through prescribed forms, effect relationships. The etymology of the English "rites" and "ritual" is suggestive of our understanding of both *li* and its cognate *ti*. In Latin, *ritus*, derives from the base **ri-* "to count", "to enumerate", which in turn is an enlargement of the base **ar-* "to join" as in "arithmetic" or "rhyme". That is, ritual practice is the rhyme and rhythm of society' (Hall and Ames 1998, p.270).

Rituals have rhyme and reason, when they make sense and provide us with a safe context for our feelings. Making things special through secular ritual is an intense creative process that explores the subtle boundaries of being human in the present, reframes the past and formulates our fears and dreams for the future.

This guide is designed for amateur ritualmakers, who need to craft a secular ceremony for themselves or for a loved one. The tools presented here have been forged, tested and tempered with individuals, couples, families and professional celebrants of diverse cultural backgrounds and language groups.

It can serve as an *aide-mémoire* for professional celebrants. If you are searching for a training course, select one that offers personal attention from a skilled instructor, a mentoring system and the stimulation and support of peers. Online instruction is popular now and useful for studying facts. Learning about accompaniment, how to deal with complex situations and preside at real ceremonies, like ritualizing, takes place during face-to-face interaction.

OUR RITUAL HERITAGE

Humankind has long felt the need to ritualize. Part I looks at the purpose, function and future of ritual in an ever-changing world. It addresses the importance of ritual identity, context and the senses for efficient ritualizing.

1

FROM ROCK ART TO RITUAL ART

In play, ritual, *and* art things [are] not ordinary – they
are less real or more real than everyday reality.

Ellen Dissanayake (1992, p.49)

Ritual is self-expanding; it opens us to energy with which to
do more ritual that opens us up to even more energy.

Michael Picucci (2005, p.51)

In a cave nestled in the remote Tsodilo Hills of Botswana's Kalahari
Desert – an area the local hunter-gatherer San tribes call the 'Rock that
Whispers – archaeologists recently found charred red arrows and a
20-foot-long stone snake as tall as a human being that was carved some
70,000 years ago. The python is surrounded by ancient rock paintings of
a giraffe and an elephant. The craft of rock art appears to have been part
of a creative process by which the San accessed spiritual power.

According to modern San myth, humankind descended from a great
python that slithered through the dry land, etching out streambeds and
hills in a ceaseless search for water. A San tribe known as the !Kung practise
a ritual they call the Giraffe Dance. As the dancers go into a trance-like
state,[1] they generate a 'body of protective spiritual energy' that extends

---

[1] During the !Kung's all night dances *num*, a 'boiling' energy, rises up through the dancer's
entire body as the dancer goes into a trance-like state called *kia*. The dancer's vision
becomes clear; he or she can see people's illnesses, see inside their bodies and even
scenes happening or that happened at great distances. *Num*, this awe-inspiring energy,
is what the healer 'puts into people' in an effort to cure them (Katz 1982, pp.42–43).

deep into the past and circulates between the dancers and the community. This power is harnessed for healing and removing societal tensions. 'Being at a dance makes our hearts happy', say the !Kung (Katz 1982, pp.xi, 34).

WHY DO WE RITUALIZE?

Why do the !Kung spend so much time on an activity that seems superfluous to survival? Why do we ritualize? Much has been written about rites and their function in society, notes ethologist Ellen Dissanayake, but one looks in vain in such studies for 'an ultimate function for ceremonial behaviour in a biological or adaptive sense' (2009, p.541). As Dissanayake watched people go about their everyday lives, she noticed that humans everywhere avidly engage in playful, artistic and ritual pursuits. 'The impetus to mark as "special" an expression or artefact, even our bodies, is deep-seated and widespread' (1992, p.60). She became convinced that these activities represent a biologically endowed need.

ATTUNEMENT, BELONGING AND IDENTITY

Dissanayake's observations of mother–infant interaction[2] shed light on the basic function of the emotional attunement[3] that helps infants survive and forms a preamble to their social bonds throughout life:

> It is not surprising that societies all over the world have developed these nodes of culture that we call ceremonies or rituals, which do for their members what mothers naturally do for babies: engage

---

2   Ellen Dissanayake states that adults in all cultures use a high-pitched, softer and breathier voice when talking to babies; this is a significant element in bonding (2000, p.30). Alfred Tomatis observed that the hearing of babies and young children is geared to the higher frequencies of women's voices (1988, p.54). Jaak Panksepp calls attention to the importance of *motherese* for language acquisition, soothing and bonding (the child's auditory system is rich in opioids). He follows this information with a story about how the singing of a female Mongolian musician helped coax a mother camel to bond with her colt (Panksepp and Biven 2012, pp.306–307).

3   Although Ellen Dissanayake uses 'mutuality', 'attachment' (2000) and 'affect attunement' (2004), 'emotional attunement' is privileged in this book to describe the secure attachment that develops first between child and carer before being reproduced in other social relationships throughout life (Scaer 2012, p.46; van der Kolk 2014, pp.111–114).

their interest, involve them in shared rhythmic pulse, and thereby install feelings of closeness and communion...which ultimately serve to hold the group together. From mutuality and belonging emerges what we call today a *sense of identity*. Arts and ritual are adaptive [behaviours] not only because they join people together in a common cause, but because they relieve anxiety. (2007; original emphasis)

MAKING SPECIAL

The pace of time changes during ritualizing – it may be slower or faster than normal time. Often, it is *bracketed off* from the rest of life, set apart or on a stage of some kind. Interestingly, these are the aspects that make ritual recognizable to us when we see it. Dissanayake dubbed the way we engage in these compelling and 'deliberately *nonordinary*' activities 'making special' (1992, pp.42–48). Throughout human history making things and activities special has engaged feeling in the most profound way. The vital concerns of the community are articulated through unusual language, repetition, exaggerated gestures, formalized or prescribed movements and stylized performance.

Coming at it from a different angle, ritual studies scholar Catherine Bell's 'profound insight was that ritual, long thought of as thoughtless action stripped of context, is more interestingly understood as strategy: a culturally strategic way of acting in the world. Ritual is a form of social activity' (Jonte-Pace 2009, p.vii). Like Dissanayake, Bell observed that ritual is a powerful and concrete way to address vital human affairs:

Exactly how this is done, how often, and with what stylistic features will depend on the specific cultural and social situation with its traditions, conventions, and innovations... In the future, we may have better tools with which to understand what people are doing when they bow their heads, offer incense to a deity, dance in masks in the plaza, or give a lecture on the meaning of ritual. Yet all these acts are ways of dealing with the world and its perceived forces and sources of power...it cannot be amiss to see in all of these instances practices that illuminate our shared humanity. (Bell 1997 [2009], pp.266–267)

RITUALMAKING: A STRATEGIC ACTIVITY

Ritual theories reflect the experiences, views and contexts of ritual theory-makers. During the Renaissance, a period that lasted roughly from the fourteenth to the seventeenth century in Europe, attitudes in Western culture became more open to the 'secular'. The knowledge that arose from humanist scholars' studies spawned greater regard for the arts, scientific discovery and humankind as a species, and challenged the influence of religious institutions. Two concepts basic to this study appeared during this period: secular and ritual.

THE CONCEPT OF THE SECULAR

Anthropologist Mary Douglas insists that secularism is just one type of worldview: it is 'an age-old cosmological type, a product of a definable social experience, which need have nothing to do with urban life or modern science...[or] transcendent explanations and powers' that can turn up in any historical age and locale (cited in Bell 1997 [2009], p.200). Anthropologist Talal Asad[4] affirms that:

> The secular is neither continuous with the religious [phase] that supposedly preceded it (that is, it is not the latest phase of a sacred origin) nor a simple break from it (that is, it is not the opposite, an essence that excludes the sacred). I take the secular to be a concept that brings together certain behaviours, knowledges, and sensibilities in modern life. (2003, p.24)

THE CONCEPT OF RITUAL

Both concepts, secular and ritual, have often been misaligned as subcategories of religion. This may be due in part to how ritual and religion have been defined.

---

4   Talal Asad ties the concept of the secular in part to the humanist teachings of the Renaissance, in part to the Enlightenment concept of nature, and in part to Hegel's philosophy of history, which allowed that the secular could embody Truth (2003, p.192).

Thinkers at the beginning of the nineteenth century gave religious ritual such a broad and inclusive definition that ritual became intrinsically tied to religion. Asad regrets that, when decoding ritual symbols, anthropologists 'incorporated theological preoccupations into an avowedly secular intellectual task' (1993, pp.55–60). Later in that century and until the beginning of the next, experts debated whether religion was rooted in myth or ritual. Early twentieth-century explorers to small tribal groups opened the ritual horizon to the influence of culture. Hard on their heels, scholars maintained that while rituals may meet a personal need for transcendence, their key role is to uphold society. As the war years shattered hearts and illusions, cognitive and symbolic systems came into vogue. Experts then predicted that, as traditional societies became modern, the spread of individualism and universal values would bring about a void in ritual. In the 1970s, theorists – among them a growing number of women – attempted to cleave ritual into religious and secular forms.

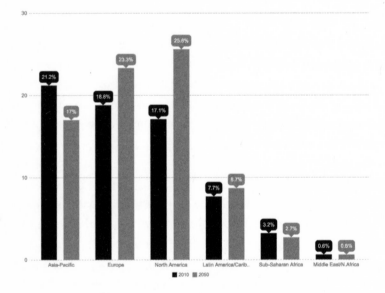

Figure 1.1. Religiously unaffiliated population, 2010 and 2050
As traditional societies become modern, adherence to hierarchical institutions drops, and the practise of ritual shifts to other domains.

Data source: Pew Research Center (2015b)

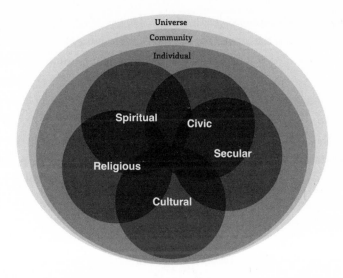

Figure 1.2. Ritual strategy: Contexts and relationships
Ritual is a culturally strategic way of acting in the world, when ritual context and relationships are coherent.

Scientific validation is now a prime criterion for scholars who tend to anatomize and dissect ritual. New definitions proliferate as it is analysed in terms of function, structure, construction and performativity. The number of adherents to traditional forms of religion is noticeably decreasing, particularly in Western cultures (see Figure 1.1). 'Yet there is really very little evidence to suggest that ritual in general declines per se. It may be more accurate to say that it shifts', affirmed Bell (1997 [2009], p.166).

The field of ritology has recently taken a quantum leap from academia to popular literature and even cyber ritual. As society becomes less and less religious and institutional control falters, ritual retains a certain aura. Ritual has wiggled off the scholar's desk to wink at us from cosmetic counters and the marquees of 'ritual spas'. It tempts us with 'a whole new way to do coffee and lunch' on our mobile apps. Why such an avid and eclectic interest in ritual in this rational age? Is ritual a fad like pet rocks, selfies and Madonna's bracelets?

In a fast-paced world, where landmarks may be fleeting, our sense of identity and belonging changes, sometimes over a few generations, sometimes more quickly. Korean–American university students who participated with their class in a Buddhist meditation were troubled when they experienced spiritual sensations they were used to feeling during Christian devotions. Those with no religious practice also experienced sensations of a spiritual character (Sutherland 2012). The students were disoriented because their feelings during the meditation were incoherent with their sense of identity and belonging. Madonna's ever-changing bracelets correspond to metamorphoses in her sense of identity and belonging. As people are affected by the impedance of the events, places and times in which they live, they adapt the ways in which they make things and activities special. Rituals like meditation, coloured bracelets, rock art and the Giraffe Dance are powerful when they are performed by and for the right people in the right context at the right time. They are confusing and disorienting when they are not right.

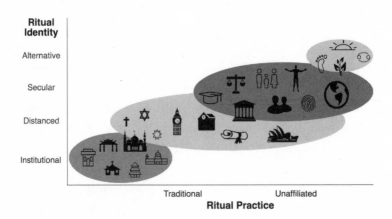

Figure 1.3. Ritual identity and practice
When ritual identity corresponds to ritual practice, emotional attunement, belonging and identity are reinforced. After identifying your ritual identity (see the *Questionnaire on ritual identity* in Chapter 5), locate your ritual practice on the chart. How does your identity and practice correspond to your need to ritualize? People with religious or *Institutional* identity and practice as well as those with *Secular* identity and practice are usually satisfied. Those with *Alternative* identity often choose spiritual practice. People with *Distanced* identity are most likely to choose rituals that do not meet their needs.

RITUAL IDENTITY

New tools and categories are needed that measure not just official religiosity, or lack of it, but ritual identity. Traditional surveys based on affiliation to institutional religions are ill suited to track ritual practice today. In Switzerland, an urbanized country with four language groups and a unique position at the crossroads of Europe, changes in the religious landscape are studied closely. A government-funded project (Stolz and Könemann 2011) based on the last few census reports uses broader and more inclusive categories than most demographers (see the Four ritual profiles box below). These four profiles take into consideration ritual practice as well as institutional membership.

Four ritual profiles

These four broad profiles of ritual identity are referred to throughout the guide:

Institutional: People who regularly practise their religion (at least once or twice a month).

Distanced: People who identify with their religion but practise occasionally (once a year or less).

Alternative: People who identify with holistic or esoteric practices.

Secular: People who identify with humanist values, and may be against religion.

Although there is no real ritual void today there is a gap, in particular, for those with Distanced or Secular identity. Those in the Distanced category[5] are by far the most challenged when it comes to meaningful ritualization. Unable to accurately measure their attachment to their religious tradition, they tend to knock on the wrong door (Religious or Secular) for a ceremony; as a result, their profound need for ritual goes unmet. The first tool in this guide, *Questionnaire on ritual identity* (see Chapter 5), was designed with the Distanced in mind. As for those in the Secular category, there are more and more competent ritual artists trained to creatively meet their need for ceremony. In the tradition of the ancient hunter-gatherers, they craft fitting ceremonies that 'make hearts happy'. Coherent ritual practice that ties the past to the present has the power to change the future.

Ceremony is 'a container for emotion, reflection and transition', affirms Tiu de Haan, an independent celebrant in London. It is 'the punctuation we need in the frenetic stream of life. A funeral is a full stop. A wedding is a plus sign. A naming ceremony is a new sentence with its own capital letter.' Rituals for other, lesser acknowledged, milestones, she describes as 'commas, or even semi-colons' (2015). We are only beginning to realize the full import of ritual in sustainable healthy living. Authentic ritual is an encounter with the senses and sensemaking; this is the subject of the next chapter.

---

5   The four profiles used in Switzerland are useful in studying *ritual identity* across cultural and religious traditions and geographical regions. The disadvantage of these categories lies in the absence of comparative data from other countries. Over the last 30 years or so, the percentage of the Swiss population that actively practises an institutional religion declined significantly, mainly due to the advancing age of adherents. In parallel, the numbers of those who consider themselves Distanced and Secular continue to increase; the younger generations are strongly represented in these last two groups. The last censuses show little variation in the Alternative population. In 2010, statistics for religious identity in Switzerland revealed: 17 per cent Institutional, 64 per cent Distanced, 10 per cent Secular and 9 per cent Alternative.
    In 2010, world census surveys indicated that over 16 per cent of the world's population is religiously unaffiliated. Concretely, this means that there are around 1.1 billion people with Distanced, Secular or Alternative profiles. Some experts predict that while the overall number of unaffiliated people around the world will decline to 13 per cent by 2050, the percentage of unaffiliated in much of Europe and North America is expected to increase: In Europe, the percentage could grow from 18 per cent in 2010 to 23 per cent in 2050. In North America it may rise from an estimated 16 per cent of the total population (including children) in 2010 to 26 per cent in 2050 (Pew Research Center 2015a).

2

THE SENSE OF RITUAL

The meaning of ritual is deep indeed.
He who tries to enter it with the kind of perception that
distinguishes hard and white, same and different, will drown there.
The meaning of ritual is great indeed.
He who tries to enter it with the uncouth and the inane
theories of the system-maker will perish there.
The meaning of ritual is lofty indeed.
He who tries to enter with the violent and arrogant ways of
those who despise common customs and consider themselves
to be above others will meet his downfall there.

Xunzi (ca. 312–ca. 220 BCE)

Making sense of ritual and making ritual that makes sense has been a challenge across the ages. Xunzi – also known as Master Xun[1] – was an early architect of Confucian philosophy and a ritualmaker during the Warring States Period (475–221 BCE). The extravagant behaviour of hierarchical systems during Xunzi's time led to armed conflict and ecological disaster

---

[1]   This translation of Xunzi's text from the Chinese is done by Burton Watson (1964, p.110). Xunzi (ca. 312– ca. 220 BCE) was a sceptic – some say atheist – secular rationalist thinker. He said: 'You pray for rain and it rains. Why? For no particular reason, I say. It is just as though you had not prayed for rain and it rained anyway.' When it rains after you pray for rain, it is just like when it rains when you didn't pray for it. Yet during a drought, officials must still pray for rain – not because it has any effect on the natural world, but because of its effect on people (IEP no date).
       Xunzi held that humans are born as egocentric beings with unquenchable desires, but they are morally perfectible. Ritual and music help people channel, moderate, and in some cases transform their desires and thus achieve partial satisfaction, and maintain social harmony (IEP no date). His educational curriculum to teach proper ritual behaviour and develop moral principles was the blueprint for traditional education in China until the modern period (Tavor 2013, p.328).

as aggressive deforestation to clear land for cultivation destroyed the
natural habitat of many plant species and decimated wildlife. In short,
it was an era characterized by fearful unrest, ecological imprudence and
rapid change – not unlike our own time.

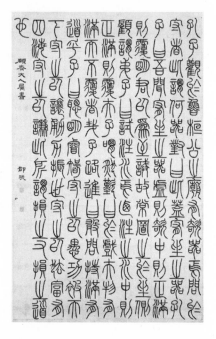

Figure 2.1. Ancient prose from the Xunzi
Written in seal script by Deng Shiru (1743–1805). Hanging scroll, ink on paper.

In reaction to the chaos, and the inadequacy of his coevals proposals,[2]
Xunzi repackaged ritual as a healthy framework for human emotion and
activity. Like most Confucians, he held that the self could be refined
through education and ritual. Ritual is consciously created by sages,
explained Xunzi, much in the same way a potter consciously creates a
pot (an object and action not part of his own nature). According to Xunzi,

---

2   Xunzi's rivals promoted meditation, ritualized sexual intercourse and gymnastic exercises.

rituals serve as a moral compass for the individual and crucial markers for the order and harmony of society. His body-based 'technology' was designed to transform people, foster an organic community and enhance sociopolitical stability (Tavor 2013, p.313).

THE HAZARDS OF OUR ULTRAMODERN ERA

Philosopher Frédéric Lenoir puts the hazards of what he dubs our 'ultra-modern' era into historical perspective:

> What our ancestors dealt with in a couple millennia, we have to grasp the significance of in a few decades. [The acceleration of change affects] our relationships to others, to nature and to spirituality... Our ancestors knew how to protect themselves. They established two 'safety zones': the first was vertical, known as God (or the gods); the second was horizontal, those first enclosures erected by villagers are the heirs of our present-day borders. We have killed the gods; we have abolished or erased our borders. It is within ourselves that we must now find these 'safety zones'. (2012, pp.62–64)

Biophysicist Peter A. Levine, formerly a NASA stress consultant, observes that both survivors of trauma and 'casualties of Western culture' may feel 'impairing disconnection from their inner sensate compasses' (2010, p.355). Like Lenoir, he encourages us to build 'islands of safety' within ourselves to keep from being overwhelmed by highly charged experiences. 'As a secular society', observes Levine,

> ...[we] are deluged with information (much of it stimulating and useful), at the same time, we suffer from a paucity of wisdom and have the desire for more personal warmth, connection and engagement...unlike in recent centuries, in which rituals have been set by hierarchical societies, we moderns need to participate

directly in the creation of our own transformational experiences through ritual. (2005, p.xvii)

Although the ritual practices of Western societies today may have little or no resemblance to the rites of the Warring States Period, the basic function of ritual has not changed. Xunzi's view of ritualizing as a meaningful activity that transforms bodies, hearts and minds of entire populations, not just individuals (Sung 2012; Tavor 2013), has growing support from the scientific community.

THE SENSES, SENSEMAKING[3] AND RITUALMAKING[4]

Until recently, scientists stuck to rational explanations; any reference whatsoever to bodies and feelings was considered too private and arcane to discuss. Over the last 25 years, the work of scientists such as Antonio and Hanna Damasio legitimizes scholarly attention to feelings. Their research reveals that pain, anger, compassion or pleasure are bodily sensations that come from our heart or guts (2003, p.4) to signify physiological need.[5] You can get behind people's emotional reactions to varied events or objects, observes Antonio Damasio, but feelings remain elusive, mysterious and inaccessible. 'Knowing about emotion, feelings and their workings does matter to how we live... I believe the new knowledge may change the

---

3   Sensemaking is the process by which people make sense of their experiences. While this process has been studied by other disciplines under other names for centuries, the term 'sensemaking' has marked scientific research since the 1970s. It is widely used today in specific social sciences such as philosophy, sociology, cognitive science and especially social psychology and interdisciplinary research programmes.

4   The term 'ritualmaking' refers to the process by which people create rituals to make sense of their life event experiences. Like the word sensemaking, it is now used by researchers and pratictioners alike.

5   'At the Brain and Creativity Institute', directors Antonio and Hanna Damasio say, 'we have been doing cross-cultural studies of emotion. At first we thought we would find very different patterns, especially with social emotions. In fact, we don't. Whether you are studying Chinese, Americans, or Iranians, you get very similar responses. There are lots of subtleties and lots of ways in which certain stimuli elicit different patterns of emotional response with different intensities, but the presence of sadness or joy is there with a uniformity that is strongly and beautifully human' (cited at http://dornsife. usc.edu/bci).

human playing field. And this is why, all things considered, in the midst of much sorrow and some joy, we can have hope' (2003, pp.287–89).

In the previous chapter we saw that Dissanayake relates emotions and the practice of ritual. 'The strong emotions elicited by the temporal arts create emotional dispositions that, in ceremonial rituals, lead to (and reinforce) cultural beliefs about the verities of one's society of intimates and to feelings of confidence and unity' (2009, p.542). Her observations have a neurological explanation.

Neurologist Robert Scaer's work on the therapeutic power of ritual in healing trauma shows that ritual practised in a group setting that feels both physically and emotionally safe is especially effective[6] (2006, p.53; 2012, p.143; 2017). Trauma fragments the mind and breaks the connections within the brain. It also seriously disrupts links between the mind and the body, trapping us in the emotions and feelings of the past (van der Kolk 2015, p.xii). The traumatized person expends a significant amount of energy just keeping it all under control, usually at the expense of concentration, memory and simply paying attention to what is happening to and around them in the present.

The sensations of trauma memory are frightening because they are inescapable and unpredictable (Levine 2015). They may be triggered without warning by anything: a sudden noise, a smell, a taste, a colour or a tone of voice, usually totally unattached to a memory of an event. The resulting inability to live fully in the present hampers adequate preparation for the future, thus wreaking havoc on health and social relationships – marriages, families and friendships (Scaer 2012, 2017). Scaer emphasizes the beneficent contribution of ritual in turning off the 'fear generator' from the past. Ritual can regularize the perception of time and

---

6   Ritualizing in the context of a group in which we feel safe meets a psychobiological need for emotional attunement, because it engages 'the same limbic brain centres – the OFC, the anterior cingulate, and the insula – that inhibit and down-regulate the amygdala. With the amygdala inhibited, intrusive thoughts are banished and homeostasis is restored and healing is promoted' (Scaer 2012, p.143; 2017). 'The potency of ritual also may explain the impact of the eye movements of EMDR, the tapping procedures of EFT and TFT (Thought Field Therapy), and the repetitive affirmative statements of the latter two approaches' (Scaer 2006, p.53; 2017).

allow people to stay in the present to experience harmonious relations (emotional attunement) with other people (2012, pp.46, 141–142, 148).

Figure 2.2. Conditions for trauma resolution and ritualizing
There are three main conditions for both effective ritualizing and the treatment of trauma: reinforce a person's sense of identity (including bodily identity), promote feelings of safety, and keep the person anchored in the present. The basic pattern for trauma resolution and authentic ritualizing is similar: whatever is done (content of ritual/treatment) must respond to a need, make sense, enhance social bonds (relationships) and be coherent with the context.

Trauma resolution and ritualizing follow similar patterns and depend on many of the same conditions (see Figure 2.2). As debilitating feelings are transformed, and the person safely reconnects with him/herself and the world, 'behaviour and even appearance' are influenced (Xunzi cited in Tavor 2013, p.316). Psychophysiological researcher Stephen Porges insists that feeling safe is essential to our wellbeing and to creative activity (2012).

Porges' landmark work *The Polyvagal Theory* (2011) expands the sociologist's toolbox with new methods for measuring emotions as they unfold during social engagement in the course of ritualization (Heinskou and Liebst 2016). Sociologist Margaret Holloway sees meaning as one of the most important aspects of contemporary ritualizing: it has to be right to feel right (2015). The situation with the Korean students in a Buddhist meditation, mentioned earlier, is an example of ritualizing that did not feel right because it was not right for *them*. Ritual that feels right and trauma resolution make use of the same the innate capacity to rebound following an overwhelming experience. This capacity is biologically linked to an animal-like surrender to the sensate world within that is capable of awakening our life force (Levine 2010, p.256). As authentic ritual grounds us in our senses, it contributes to healing but also to the prevention or renegotiation of trauma.

> Ritualizing a lifecycle passage, or even a seasonal event, serves as a benchmark or reference point among a series of lesser points. It reassures us that we have indeed moved on from one phase to another, and that the transition has truly been completed. It inaugurates a new reality within which we can evolve in peace.
>
> *Smyth (2014)*

THE HUMANIZING EFFECT OF RITUALS

Do not do to others what you do not want done to yourself.
The Golden Rule, espoused by Confucius and Xunzi

Xunzi describes the humanizing effect of ritual as a safe framework for expressing and harnessing strong and potentially dangerous emotions in a harmonious and fulfilling manner (Kline 2004, p.203). There are striking similarities between Xunzi's descriptions of how feelings become vehicles for positive change and what I have observed as a celebrant during secular ceremonies, particularly in funerals. The attention span of the assembly is short. People do not stay long with an emotion; they spontaneously oscillate between pain and pleasure. Tears and laughter may follow in rapid succession. An overwhelming sense of absence may be replaced by a joyful memory, followed by the unacceptable sight of their loved one in a coffin, and the warmth of a friend's hand... There are signs of physical release or discharge: a deep breath, moist eyes, yawning, a trembling in the face, lips or hands, or movements that stretch muscles in the shoulders, neck, hands, or legs. As the ceremony draws to a close, people glance around, as though they are waking up and reorienting themselves to the room and the people around them. Their movements are not as stiff; there is less tension in their faces.

When the ceremony flows in a gentle, harmonious manner, people feel supported. Later, they may speak of a gut-level sense of relief or of feeling at peace. They have moved on to new place in their grief where they live without their loved one. Fitting ritualization contains the emotions of the past in the past, and firmly anchors people physically and sensorily in the present, thus opening the way for a new future.

Although Levine has never applied to funerals the oscillation he prescribed for the resolution of trauma,[7] he does recognize that 'the tranquil feelings of aliveness and ecstatic self-transcendence that make us fully human can also be accessed through ritual. This way they become enduring features of our existence' (2005, p.xvii).

We ritualize for many reasons, not the least of which is to feel safe. 'What would it be like if creative people felt safe, or...more people could

---

7   Peter A. Levine refers to this moving back and forth between emotions as pendulation, 'the primal rhythm expressed as movement from constriction to expansion – and back to constriction, but gradually opening to more and more expansion... The perception of pendulation guides the gradual contained release (discharge) of "trauma energies" leading to expansive body sensations and successful trauma resolution' (2010, p.80). He encourages 'titrating' emotion (keep it at a low level and go slowly). The acronym TRIPODs describes this process in healing trauma: Titrating, Resourcing, Integrating, Pendulating, Organizing, Discharging, Stabilizing.

become creative if they felt safe', Porges asks (2012)?[8] Today, as in Xunzi's time, we need this creativity to repackage ritual as alternative technology of the body–heart–mind that is capable of transforming people, fostering an organic communal body and enhancing social and geopolitical stability. The meaning of ritual is lofty indeed.

 See *Five techniques for feeling safe* in Chapter 5.

---

8 'Porges helped us understand how dynamic our biological systems are and gave us an explanation why a kind face and a soothing tone of voice can dramatically alter the entire organization of the human organism – that is, how being seen and understood can help shift people out of disorganised fearful states... If physiological mind-brain-viscera communication is the royal road to affect regulation, this invites a radical shift in our therapeutic approaches...to anxiety, attention deficit/hyperactivity disorder, autism, and trauma-related psychopathology... The polyvagal theory legitimates the study of age-old collective and religious [sic] practices such as communal chanting, various breathing technics, and other methods that shifts in autonomic state' (van der Kolk 2011, p.xvi).

RITUAL THROUGH CRAFT

Ritualmaking is a powerful craft that can shape people and transform the future. Making things and participating in activities comes naturally to us. Like many ancient occupations, the craft of ritualmaking has been neglected but not abandoned. Traditional methods open the way for new solutions to meet humankind's need for effective ritual today.

Part II looks at the basics of the craft of ritualizing. Crafting ritual is a profoundly human activity that involves the mind, the body and even the viscera in a process that takes us to the heart of reality.

Please read Part II before ritualizing a specific event presented in Part III.

3

GUIDELINES FOR RITUALIZING

Necessity is the mother of invention.

Proverb attributed to Plato (428–348 BCE)

How did our ancestors come up with rituals powerful enough to last through the ages? How can we create rituals today that meet our needs and make sense? We are not born ritualmakers. Or are we?

THE CRAFT OF RITUALMAKING

Although we have little explicit knowledge of how rituals were created by our ancestors, anthropologist Matthieu Smyth points out that ritualization was not always left to specialists (2015, personal communication). In early, less hierarchical cultures, hunter-gatherer groups like the San tribes shared ritualmaking or assumed it informally on an ad hoc basis. Throughout most of recorded history, rituals – just like footwear, hats, pots and fabric – were crafted by people. While not all of these objects were aesthetically pleasing, even the simplest article was ruggedly functional. As the industrial revolution took hold in the mid-1800s, attitudes towards handcrafted products changed radically. Values like quality, originality, functionality and durability gave way to new criteria such as production speed, reproducibility, low prices and programmed obsolescence. Industry inflated cities and pushed people to specialize. Machines manufactured objects and people became consumers. In a similar process, ritualmaking gradually became the affair of hierarchical institutions and their members became end users.

We cannot claim an unbroken lineage of ritual sages and artisans, and no one thought to leave us an instruction booklet. Even so, just as our ancestors made foot coverings to protect their feet from the elements, our aptitude for creating our own ritual grows with our need. Yet, although most people can sew a button on a shirt, not everyone is a dressmaker. In the same way, nearly anyone can make rituals but not everyone is a ritual artisan. Both the amateur and the professional may be efficient and do quality work. The main difference lies in the artisan's experience, proficiency and the fact that he or she is remunerated for the work. Furthermore, in most traditions, the artisan upholds a social obligation to work towards the spiritual and material welfare of society. All craftspeople require discipline, creativity, a few guidelines, appropriate tools, and perhaps a good checklist.

GUIDELINES FOR RITUALIZING

AUTHENTICITY, NOT PARODY

Meaningful ritual is based on genuine intention and performance. Culture has long been enriched by the exchange of ideas, yet borrowing rituals from other people's traditions rarely makes sense and can be seen as disrespectful. Some of my colleagues are regularly solicited for indigenous rituals. People who are distanced from their tradition of origin are most challenged when it comes to the ritualizing of a life event (see the *Questionnaire on ritual identity* in Chapter 5). 'I am the only one who can tell the story of my life and say what it means' says Dorothy Allison (1996, p.70). This applies to ritual in particular. It has to be right to feel right; using our own objects, symbols and language provides the best base for crafting authentic ritual.

> **Declaration of war against exploiters of Lakota spirituality**
>
> Traditional leaders of several tribes have declared war on those who usurp ritual elements of their spiritual tradition:
>
> Whereas for too long we have suffered the unspeakable indignity of having our most precious Lakota ceremonies and spiritual practices desecrated, mocked and abused by non-Indian 'wannabes', hucksters, cultists, commercial profiteers and self-styled 'New Age shamans' and their followers... Whereas with horror and outrage we see this disgraceful expropriation of our sacred Lakota traditions has reached epidemic proportions in urban areas... We hereby and henceforth declare war against all persons who persist in exploiting, abusing, and misrepresenting the sacred traditions and spiritual practices of the Lakota, Dakota and Nakota people.
>
> *The People's Paths* (1993)

VOLUNTARY, NOT IMPOSED

A Christian lighting a votive candle or a Buddhist burning incense requires little or no explanation for the gesture. Even those who know little about their tradition find the act meaningful on several levels. As we have seen in Chapters 1 and 2, the significance of such an act may be transferrable to non-religious settings. Such an act can also arouse confusing or ambivalent feelings. This is a risk for rituals that are foisted on people without their input or consent.

Historically oppressed peoples who have been excluded from ritualmaking processes are particularly sensitive to imposed rituals. Peace-builder Lisa Schirch recounts how a candle-lighting ritual devised by the staff of a youth camp fell flat for the participants from opposing sides of the Cypriot conflict. None of the youth seemed involved as they came to the front of the room, lit a candle and shared a phrase that was supposed to express their dreams or wishes for the future. There was minimal enthusiasm during the singing of 'Imagine' by John Lennon. 'The song and the ritual ended in giggles, a few claps, and people straggling away,' remembers Schirch. 'Then one camper asked everyone to stand up and shout "WE WANT PEACE!" together three times in a row. Excited clapping, hoots, hollers, and laughter followed, ending the ritual on a positive note' (2005, p.168).

At the end of a wedding ceremony at which I presided, the best man pulled me aside to express his appreciation. 'My wife and I also hired a celebrant for our wedding ceremony. The celebrant proposed three union rituals. We were the least uncomfortable with having our hands wrapped in a scarf, so we chose that one. Our celebrant and our friends talked about what they thought marriage should mean to us, while we sat there with this scarf over our hands. We felt like accessories at our own wedding. Today, it wasn't like that. My friends were at the centre of their wedding ceremony. Yes, that's it! You held the frame and my friends – all of us – were in the picture. It was very moving.'

THERAPEUTIC, NOT THERAPY

Over 2000 years ago, Xunzi perceived ritual as a meaningful, even therapeutic, experience that gratifies the senses, when it is performed in a controlled setting with a clear agenda in mind. Ritualizing emotionally charged situations such as a funeral for a mother of young children or a father who committed suicide, a wedding of a couple facing unemployment or a naming ceremony for a terminally ill child can indeed have a salutary effect. Ritual may deal with the emotions generated in a therapeutic manner, but therapy is not the end purpose of ritual. Psychotherapy is about treatment of dis-ease: mitigating troublesome behaviours, beliefs, compulsions, thoughts or emotions. The reason why we ritualize should not be confused with the possible benefits such as healing, feeling more peaceful, resolving family issues, consolidating a couple's relationship or finding a new job. There are other, more direct and efficient, means of dealing with these situations. Although the desired outcomes may be similar, intention and process are quite different. Ritualizing is often therapeutic, but it should not be confused with therapy.

THEATRICAL, NOT THEATRE

A few months before they were to marry, a couple organizing a medieval-themed wedding in an old castle asked me for help, because they were at a loss as to how to handle the ceremony. They had everything they needed, except for the content. We first addressed who would be marrying whom: Would it be the marriage of a medieval page and a lady-in-waiting, or that of a couple of twenty-first-century students who happened to be dressed in wedding clothes from another age? How would it feel to them? How would their guests know what kind of support the couple expected of them in the future? To reduce the risk of the ceremony becoming what the couple referred to as a 'blatant pastiche', they wrote their own vows, made a few other adjustments to the programme, and invited a trusted friend to preside and explain their intentions.

Figure 3.1. 1 November commemorations of the dead
The traditional visit to a loved-one's grave is ritualized in the evening in a Dutch cemetery using a long table dressed in old lace, odd dishes and salvaged cutlery. There are phrases written on the plates.
© Ida van der Lee

PLAYFUL, NOT A GAME

Cooperation and teamwork are key to a ceremony's success. Each player has a role and must respect the rules. During our trainings for celebrants, an actor works with participants on the use of space and even strategy, as well as on voice, diction and scenography. Ritualization can be light-hearted and playful, but it is not a game; it is for real.

TIME-OUT-OF-TIME, NOT TIME-OUT

During a ceremony we may feel a salutary time-out-of-time: we are present but may lose track of time because it seems to accelerate or slow down. Both traditional and emerging secular rituals can produce this sense of slipping from an ordinary to an extraordinary time where feelings are richer and more intense than usual. Even when the content of a ceremony itself is not particularly emotional, the event (birthday) or setting (funeral parlour) may induce strong feelings.

Have you ever walked out of a wedding or a funeral? Do you know why? In normal circumstances, the brain's timekeeper keeps us conscious of the fact that whatever is happening – good or bad – will sooner or later end. During an event that is too stressful – be it happy or sad – the brain's timekeeper[1] can go offline. This kind of time-out is not very pleasant. Yet as soon as we can stretch, smile, yawn or heave a sigh of relief, our timekeeper resets, and we return to normal time.

CELEBRATION, NOT A PARTY

Life event ceremonies may not all be festive but they are all bittersweet. A wedding may be more sweet than bitter, a funeral more bitter than sweet. Ideally, the bitterness of the occasion is sweetened by the presence of well-meaning people, words of sympathy and acts of kindness. For this reason, the social gathering is an extension of the ceremony itself; the support manifested there represents long-term commitment.

---

[1]   The scientific name for the timekeeper is the dorsolateral prefrontal cortex (DLPFC). It is responsible for 'telling us how our present experience relates to the past and how it may affect the future' (van der Kolk 2014, p.69).

Parents who wanted to mark their son's coming of age organized a surprise party with his friends. Shortly afterwards the young man left home for university. After completing his first year, he told his parents that he finally felt like an adult. University did what neither his graduation ceremony nor his birthday party had done for him. A social gathering alone can celebrate but not ritualize an occasion.

WASTE NOT, WANT NOT

Although few organizers even think of working towards zero waste, most celebrations typically produce significant quantities of rubbish and waste materials. 'How many times are we going to get married?!' 'So what if our carbon imprint[2] is high, just this once.' 'What's a birthday party without balloons?' 'Who wants to wash dishes after their grandparents' anniversary dinner?' You don't need to be a tree-hugging environmentalist to reduce waste – even for a celebration. It makes sense not only for the planet, but also for us all. Take up the challenge by concentrating on just one area where you will effectively reduce waste. Use your imagination and creativity. You may well find that there are more advantages than disadvantages to your choices.

Travel

Reduce the distance your guests will need to travel in motor vehicles. Choose a venue for the wedding ceremony that is close to the reception. One couple hired a bus to bring their out-of-town guests from the hotel to the wedding venue. No one had to worry about finding the venue or about driving unfamiliar roads in the dark after the festive part of the celebration. The same attitude may apply to other events. One family organized their son's funeral in the gym of the village school. The caterers set the reception up while the mourners attended the burial at the village cemetery.

----

2   What is a 'carbon imprint'? Sometimes referred to as a 'carbon footprint', it is a measure of how much more CO_2 a person uses than is replaced by natural processes or personal environmental action. A multi-language website, www.myclimate.org, calculates the carbon imprint for different activities and modes of transport.

Tableware

Consider the impact of plastic decorations, plates and cutlery. Suitable solutions exist now, such as compostable, recyclable, biodegradable tableware and party decorations that are less toxic for the environment.

Decorations and fun

The rice traditionally thrown at weddings can be replaced by birdseed or even wildflower seeds. One family decorated the tables at their reception with garden flowers they placed in painted shoe boxes.

Balloons are cheerful and evoke happy memories for most people. Two types of balloons are widely in use: latex and Mylar. Mylar nylon balloons are often coated with a metallic finish; they are not classified as biodegradable and do not decompose. Latex (natural rubber) takes about six months to decompose. Fish, fowl and other animals may die if they ingest bits or get caught in the strings tied to balloons. Neither kind of balloon (Mylar/latex) should be filled with helium and launched on account of the risks to the environment.

The following can be used as alternative decorations:

- Latex balloons can be blown up the old-fashioned way, used in a controlled setting, and then composted.

- Tie ribbons onto sticks – for dancing around.

- Use bubbles made of liquid soap.

- Craft things – like origami – from old newspapers and magazine pages.

- Musical instruments can be made from recycled materials.

The next chapter looks at ritual materials and design.

4

RITUAL MATERIALS AND DESIGN

Whereas in traditional ritual settings one may move smoothly from the planning phase to ritualizing, contemporary secular ritualmaking requires a significant creative phase. The creative process grows out of our human need to mark an occasion or a life event as being special. Primal ritual materials include people, participation and place; from these three sources come the words, gestures and objects that anchor ritual in reality. Contemporary secular ritual makes sense when it is designed around these materials, all of which must be coherent with the values of the people or the occasion at the centre of the ritual.

Jeltje Gordon-Lennox

Good materials and design are essential for the success of architects, artisans and crafters of ritual alike. The Bauhaus architect Mies van der Rohe said, 'No design is possible until the materials with which you design are completely understood' (cited in Borden 2010, p.7). He encouraged people to look at these aspects in terms of their function and broader context:

> We must remember that everything depends on how we use a material, not on the material itself... Each material is only what we make of it... And, just as we acquaint ourselves with materials,

just as we must understand functions,[1] so we must become familiar with the psychological and spiritual factors of our day. No cultural activity is possible otherwise; for we are dependent on the spirit of our time. (Mies 1938)

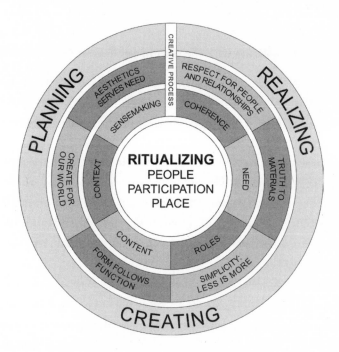

Figure 4.1. The creative process
This diagram, inspired by the Bauhaus movement, illustrates the importance of design and materials in the creative process of crafting ritual.

In a similar manner, rituals studies expert Ronald L. Grimes warns against grafting elements we do not understand into our rituals, because we will end up with rituals that we cannot fully absorb. This is particularly true when it comes to traditional rituals that have little or no connection

---

1   Mies van der Rohe's ideas were not new, but they were adapted to the spirit of his time. Carlo Lodoli (1690–1761), an Italian architectural theorist and mathematician, anticipated modernist notions of functionalism and truth to materials. His architectural forms and proportions were derived from the abilities of the materials used.

with our own lives. So many layers of meaning will remain hidden from us that it cannot feel right. More to the point, we do not need others' rituals to give meaning to our celebrations. Nudging out the sense of an occasion and showing what it means to us with our words, objects and symbols is revealed in the creative process.

Grimes: Ritualizing with the stuff in our drawers

Some rituals are not much more than sugary confections, all tantalization and immediate gratification, but ultimately leaving us starved for real meaning. Pilfering other people's rituals can turn into a spiritual imperialism that mirrors Western culture's historic sense of ownership of the world. One of the reasons we might become interested in the rituals of hunter-gatherer societies is because we are moving around a lot, like hunters and gatherers. But our sense of connection with space and our sense of loyalty to a particular place have changed; our ritual sensibility has changed as well.

Like traditional rituals, do-it-yourself (DIY) ritual can result in complicity, empty gestures, people having to do something they resist doing. In either case, deep-seated resentment can lie under the surface of ritual acts. If DIY rituals are really going to meet our needs, they have to be made up out of the familiar, not the exotic: metaphors that make sense to us, language that reflects the way we see the world, and symbols with which we have a history. Start with your own broken teacups, the stuff in your backyard, keepsakes in the backs of drawers. Begin there, not with someone else's rituals.

Grimes (2016)

RITUAL MATERIALS

People, participation and place represent the three main categories for ritual materials. Remember that everything depends on how we use a material, not on the material itself. Consider how this person or that place might best serve your ritual design.

PEOPLE

As the centre person, a craftsperson or a participant in a ceremony, you are your main resource: who you are, your hopes and fears, your ties to those present, your life experience, books you have read, films you appreciate, food you like to eat, anything that has meaning to you in this context, all of this makes for rich material in ritualmaking.

PARTICIPATION

Ritual is realized through participation. Whether a ritual is carried out by one person or hundreds of people, their participation is essential. People participate through their presence, language and gestures. They experience and make sense of ritual using all of their senses. Objects too can participate by simply being there.

PLACE

'Place' refers to how a ceremony fits into our lives as well as to the physical aspects such as setting, the space occupied by people and things and the time in which ritual is enacted. Suitability depends entirely on what makes sense and is coherent with the essence of the ceremony.

RITUAL DESIGN

SIX PILLARS OF DESIGN

Ritualmaking is buttressed by six supports: need, context, roles, content, sensemaking and coherence.

Need

The *raison d'être* of ritualizing is our profound human need. Most of the time this need is obvious. Nonetheless, it helps to identify it early in the creative process. Sometimes the need for appropriate ritual may not be met until years later. When a mountain-climber, a firm atheist, fell to his death, his family numbly went through the motions of a religious funeral. Twenty-five years later they gathered for a memorial ceremony on the spot where he died. Afterwards, the deceased's now adult son remarked: 'I agreed to this ceremony to please my mother. I now realize how important it was for us all to talk about who our father really was, feel our loss and mourn the fact that we had to grow up without him.'

Context

Adequate understanding of context is crucial – effective ritualizing is influenced by the impedance of place and time. Context variables include ritual identity, time and timing, place and space, roles and relationships, signs and symbols, language and communication.

A couple who wanted a non-religious naming ceremony for their newborn with sponsors from various cultural traditions reserved a desacralized chapel for a Sunday in June and chose water as their symbol. They all wrote lovely promises for the baby. A week before the ceremony, the couple did an about-face and in record time organized a traditional Catholic baptism. What happened here? It turned out that the ambiguity of the physical context (place, date, symbols, date) reflected the parents' reticence to confront their differing ritual identities and levels of attachment to tradition. It also deflected their families' attention from the couple's plans for a non-religious ceremony. Unprepared to deal with the outcry, the parents ceded to family expectations.

In what at first glance seems like a similar situation, a refugee family asked me to help them mark the arrival of their third child with a secular ceremony. They explained: 'We now speak a new language in a new place with new people who practise different customs. A traditional ceremony does not fit us anymore.' The welcome ceremony, based on the values that carried the family through their ordeal, celebrated the arrival of their child, and anchored them even more firmly in their new context.

Roles

Attributing the right roles to the right people requires an accurate grasp of the context. In the first case described above, the parents found a secular context appealing because they could choose their closest friends to be the child's sponsors – a Catholic baptism requires Catholic godparents. Four main roles must be identified in secular ritual (see Figure 4.2): the person, people or relationship at the centre of the occasion, the craftspeople, the presider, and people who participate actively or as observers.

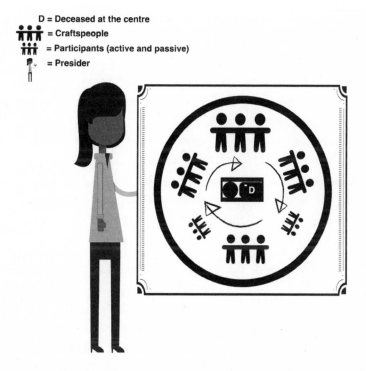

Figure 4.2. Four principal roles
In a funeral, the life of the deceased is at the centre of the ritual, the craftspeople are represented by the larger figures, the participants by the smaller figures and the presider holds the frame around the ceremony.

In the case of a wedding, the couple's relationship is at the centre of a ritual that they craft together. Friends and family participate actively or by their presence, while a third person presides. In a ritual that honours a separation, the relationship is again at the centre. The crafter and presider can be the same person; others may attend or be invited to attend in spirit but not be physically present.

Content

The content of a ceremony unpacks and conveys what is at the heart of the ritual. Elements such as meaningful words, gestures, music and objects constitute the content.

Content

The temporal arts are integral to ceremonies because, by elaborating their sources in affiliative behaviour, participants gain a felt sense of social identity (as in rites of passage) and identification (of belonging to their group). Additionally, through the temporal arts, ceremonies instil in individuals a sense of meaningfulness and significance of their group's messages and a felt sense of competence that the important and uncertain matters of the ritual can be dealt with. Belonging, meaning and competence are vital human emotional needs, and the temporal arts in ritual ceremonies help individuals achieve and sustain them.

Dissanayake (2009, p.542)

Sensemaking

Making ritual that feels right involves *seeking, creating* and *taking meaning* (Holloway 2015). People *seek meaning* through their choices about the different aspects of the ceremony such as music, readings, dress, symbols and memorials. They then use these elements to *create meaning* for themselves and those present at the ceremony. *Taking meaning* from a ceremony helps mark the transition and anchors it in our daily life. In the case of a wedding, the couple *seek meaning* as they make choices about the venue, the content of ceremony, who participates and who is invited. They *create meaning* out of their love for each other. With their families and friends as witnesses, they *take meaning* from the ceremony. Everyone present is anchored in a new reality.

Coherence

Coherence is the glue that holds all the elements of ritual together. There is coherence when (1) need and expectations are clear, (2) the roles are played by the right people, (3) in the right context, (4) expressed with suitable content (5) that conveys meaning. For example, instead of wedding rings they would not wear, watchmakers sealed their vow with watches they made for each other. A couple working in a humanitarian organization chose to marry on a boat named for Henry Dunant (1828–1910), founder of the Red Cross. One woman turned the old insult 'crone' on its head to honour her passage into the third phase of her life with a croning ceremony, saying that this honoured a rebellious streak in her personality.

SIX RULES FOR RITUAL DESIGN

These basic rules of design form the acronym 'CRAFTS'.

Create for our world

Time-honoured ritual elements – such as fire, water or salt – do not in and of themselves communicate meaning. If used, they must be introduced in a way that makes for ready and accurate interpretation to those assembled. A young couple wordlessly introduced bread and wine into their non-religious wedding ceremony and left their guests with the task of making sense of the traditionally religious symbols in this context. A multicultural couple chose the theme 'the spices in our life' for their wedding ceremony; they closed it with a few words about why they served their guests toast rounds spread with spices from their respective countries. Everything that is brought into the ceremony will enhance meaning or be counter-productive. Craftspeople anticipate misinterpretation by fixing the elements of the ceremony firmly in their present, without neglecting their past. Our dependence on the spirit of our time comes through in this pivotal phase of the creative process. It is what gives secular ritual the power to transform the future.

Respect for people and relationships

Harmonious ritualization respects people (present and absent), their relationships and interrelationships. The best-known summary of respect is the Golden Rule, which, in essence, means 'do no harm to oneself or others'. In the case of the confusing wedding ritual described above, a brief explanation might have made sense of the couple's use of traditional symbols – and put people at ease. Unlike animals, we need words to transmit the sense of our acts. When we choose to ritualize with keepsakes in the backs of our drawers, it is often easier to convey their meaning in a simple manner. Due regard for the feelings, wishes, rights and traditions of others strengthens social bonds.

Aesthetics serves need

'Aesthetics', a word derived from the Greek, refers to how we apprehend beauty through our senses, perception and feelings. Taking this a step further, an anthropologist of African art talks about the 'affecting presence' of artefacts and ceremonies (cited in Dissanayake 1988 [2002], p.59). A couple who hired a gospel singer to perform at their wedding ceremony showed signs of discomfort about five minutes into the improvisation. They asked me to get her to cut it short. The music definitely had an affecting presence. Even so, in this couple's wedding, it drew everyone's attention away from – rather than towards – the newly-weds because it reflected neither their taste in music nor their relationship. Affecting presence is essential to meaningful ritualizing; 'art for art's sake'[2] feels out of place when it does not enhance sensemaking.

---

2   'Art for art's sake' or '*l'art pour l'art*', a slogan credited to Théophile Gautier (1811–72), was a reaction among Western artists against the idea that art had to serve some practical, moral or didactic purpose. It presents art as an independent and well-defined domain in itself that is solely concerned with aesthetics, imagination, enjoyment and

Form follows function

'Form follows function', a main tenet of Bauhaus ideology, expresses the reaction of the movement against design that hides the essence of an object under complex forms. In this context, the phrase is a reminder that ceremony's design must be functional: the essence should be clear and any object that is introduced should be used. It would be incongruous to have a photo of anyone but the deceased at a funeral. The ring bearer expects that the rings he or she ceremoniously bears will be placed on the newly-weds' hands. Ecologically minded parents will invite their guests to the park rather than the playroom of a fast-food chain.

Truth to materials

A carpenter trues-up rough wood by working it until it is square, flat and smooth. Ritual craftspeople, like carpenters, must true-up their materials. Truth to materials begins with using the right person in the right place to say or do the right thing at the right time.

Simplicity: Less is more

Although simplicity is a deceptively demanding art form, the ritualmaker – whether beginner or advanced – is encouraged to employ a simple design and stick to basic forms. The heart of the ritualization stands out best in a simple ceremony. During life event celebrations, emotion tends to run high, making it hard for people to concentrate. An outdoor ceremony compounds the number of distractions. Complex concepts or ideas become difficult, if not impossible, to grasp. Understanding of the essence of the event is reinforced through repetition and short concise interventions in multiple art forms that appeal to the senses.

During one of my first experiences as a wedding celebrant, I lost the flow of what was supposed to be a 15-minute outdoor ceremony where

---

the self-expression of the artist. George Sand and Friedrich Nietzsche criticized the slogan claiming that art 'for art's sake' just does not exist. Postcolonial African writers such as Leopold Senghor and Chinua Achebe consider the phrase a Eurocentric view on art and creation.

everyone was standing. The best man's endless stories about the groom and his ex-partners were followed by a skit by the maid of honour and her children. As the dignity of the moment evaporated, the newly-weds, their parents and the guests became impatient and embarrassed. The right people contributed at the right place, but the materials were out of true with the couple's sense of commitment and the timing. The couple and I should have worked during the creating phase to simplify and true-up these contributions.

THE CREATIVE PROCESS

All ritualizing involves a planning and a realizing phase. In traditional ritualizing these two are the main phases. The work of interpreting the meaning of the occasion has already been done, usually by an institution. What sets the craft of ritualmaking apart is the creating phase. Why is it important to use our creative power? Journalist and author Brenda Ueland answers: 'Because there is nothing that makes people so generous, joyful, lively, bold and compassionate, so indifferent to fighting and the accumulation of objects and money' (1938 [2010], p.155). Emerging ritual offers an opportunity to explore, create and make sense of an occasion – to make it special.

PLANNING PHASE

> Quis, quid, quando, ubi, cur, quem ad modum, quibus adminiculis.[3]
> *Hermagoras of Temnos (ca. 100 BCE)*

The planning phase involves four of Hermgoras' seven questions: who, what, where and when? This is the time for brainstorming. Even if you are sure that you want to hold a naming ceremony for your youngest in the backyard on Saturday 23 May at 4 o'clock, note down a few other options,

---

3   Hermagoras of Temnos, a first-century Greek rhetor, is said to have used the method of dividing a topic into its 'seven circumstances' (who, what, when, where, why, in what way, by what means). His approach inspired the '5 Ws' used widely in journalism, education and police investigation.

in pencil. Give yourself permission to change your mind. It may save you time in the long run. During the creating phase, test your choices for coherence. This extra step is a safeguard to ensure that your choices correspond to your needs.

Risk factors for the planning phase

The greatest risk in this first phase lies in unexpressed, and thus unmet, expectations. Misunderstandings are often due to lack of communication or to giving people unsuitable roles. Leave time for the unexpected. Make contingency plans for inclement weather.

CREATING PHASE

The creating phase addresses Hermagoras' three other questions: why, in what way, by what means? Why are you ritualizing this occasion? How do you imagine it? What means will you use? This phase represents the fundamental difference between ready-made and handcrafted rituals. Take your time. Creation is not about *giving* the occasion meaning or about what it *should* mean; it is about uncovering *what it means to you*. Set aside ideas of what your ceremony should look like. Maybe what you create will be totally different from anything you have seen elsewhere, or maybe it will be similar. Gloria Steinem tells us to 'create the means that best reflect the ends we want. Try to make each moment authentic, and you'll get to an authentic end' (2012, n.p.). The goal is not originality but simplicity, truthfulness and authenticity.

Risk factors for the creating phase

It is tempting to buy a pile of books or spend hours on the internet to see what others wrote and did in their ceremony. Trust yourself. Look at how others went about it *after* you have decided what you want to write or do. If you so desire, you may use others' material; most people find their choices confirmed.

Surprises, including improvised contributions, can confuse or overwhelm people. They are welcome at the reception but not appropriate for the ceremony.

REALIZING PHASE

The shared experience of the ceremony – even if it is only a few words – launches an event. The ceremony is a way of letting members of a group know what the others know. This lends a sense of cohesion to an often disparate group. Ritualizing offers those present an opportunity to gradually and gently weave *new meaning* – no matter how bittersweet – into the fabric of daily life. Author Rita Mae Brown believes 'that we often disguise pain through ritual and it may be the only solace we have' (1988, n.p.). Ritual provides a comfort, and it inaugurates a new reality within which all of the participants can evolve in peace.

Risk factors for the realizing phase

On the day of the event, speakers should arrive early and prepared. Guests appreciate being greeted with water or fruit juice, especially in hot weather. Reserve alcoholic drinks for the social gathering. People who are already in party mode cannot be attentive during the ceremony. The presider is solely responsible for carrying the ceremony and respecting the time frame.

Before moving on to look at the tools of ritual, it is important to remind ourselves why we embark on this creative adventure. Anthropologist Barbara Myerhoff said: '[Ritual] dwells in an invisible reality and gives this reality a vocabulary, props, costume, gesture, scenery. Ritual makes things separate, sets them apart from ordinary affairs and thoughts. Rituals need not be solemn, but they are formalized, stylized, extraordinary, and artificial. In the name of ritual, we can do anything. We can do astonishing acts. In the end, ritual gives us assurance about the unification of things' (cited in Broner 1999, p.37).

5

A RITUAL TOOLBOX

Figure 5.1. A ritual toolbox

As you create meaningful rituals to celebrate the important events in your life, you want practical tools that work with you rather than for you: tools that help you express that meaning with your own words; tools that help you identify the personal experiences, cultural traditions, stories and objects that make sense to you in this context.

Jeltje Gordon-Lennox

'People need new Tools to work with rather than new Tools that work for them', claimed Ivan Illich (1973, p.10). This is also true for contemporary ritualizing. Practical knowledge of ritualmaking begins with an introduction to some basic tools. Our attitude towards those tools affects how we use them.

American artist Toshio Odate was apprenticed as a youth to a *shokunin* (artisan) in Japan to learn the sliding-door-maker's trade. He compares the Japanese attitude towards tools with the modern approach he encountered in the West:

> Though the Japanese tools often look simple when compared to Western tools, they are really very complicated to use, performing best through the *shokunin*'s preparation, ability and experience... in America especially, knowledge of new things is often gained through experimentation... I realize it is a natural outgrowth of interest and respect for personal opinion, not recklessness or carelessness. (1998, p.1)

Instead of ready-made rituals, this chapter proposes a toolbox of plain functional tools designed to work with you rather than for you. As you create unique rituals for your life, use your own tradition – it is very complicated to use and performs best in your expert hands. Experiment too; use this modern approach to underscore what is important for you as you ritualize today.

This ritual toolbox is organized into compartments that correspond to the three phases of the crafting process. Specific tools are recommended for each of the ceremonies in Part III. Nonetheless, you should use each of the tools whenever and wherever they suit the task at hand, just as you would the tools in your toolbox at home.

THE CHECKLIST

The checklist forms the backbone of this handbook. 'The list is the origin of culture', Umberto Eco asserted. 'The list doesn't destroy culture; it creates it... It allows us to question the essential definitions... We like lists because we don't want to die' (2009). The really important things should not be left to memory, particularly under conditions of complexity, as in ritualizing. Checklists are *required* for success, affirms surgeon Atul Gawande (2011, p.79). His surgery checklist asks team members to introduce themselves to each other and then agree – together, in advance – what is to be done and who takes control if things go belly-up. When it was tested in eight pilot medical centres around the world, major complications for surgical patients fell 36 per cent and mortality dropped by 47 per cent. Imagine the success of a medicament – exempt of side-effects – effective on this scale!

An early form of the *Checklist for a Funeral Ceremony* worked for grandchildren who needed to 'do something' to take leave of their beloved grandmother. It got them to work together and focus on their common goals. A checklist is invaluable in situations where people nurse long-standing feuds; it does not take sides. The *Checklist for a Wedding Ceremony* got couples to fix their attention on their ceremony, and let their divorced parents decide who would sit next to whom. While a checklist is no substitute for common sense and skill, and it *does not list everything one should do*, it does guide craftspeople as they identify what is at the heart of the ceremony by obliging them to pause and communicate with each other. The true beauty of the checklist lies in how it makes the members of the team communicate and assume responsibility – and credit – for the end result.

READ–DO CHECKLISTS

The list used in this handbook is referred to as a READ–DO checklist: the essential elements are identified, created and then put together in a certain order. These checklists have a common structure and function. Each of the three columns in the checklist evokes an action in the creative process *plan, create, realize.*

CHECKLIST FUNCTION

1. *Identify* the essential elements and *accomplish* the main steps.

2. *Enforce pauses* during which those directly responsible can talk to each other about *what is at the heart of the occasion FOR THEM.*

3. Help the craftspeople (a) *feel like a team*, (b) *decide in advance what to do* and (c) *who takes control if things do not go as planned.*

4. Ensure that other *lists are made and used* (e.g. wedding list: bridal bouquet, programme, rings...).

RISK FACTORS IN USING A CHECKLIST

While the efficacy of the checklist has been proven time and again, using it seems to go against a myth about how successful people function: the truly great are daring; they improvise, they do not need protocols and checklists. 'Maybe our idea of heroism needs updating' concedes Gawande (2011, p.173). Checklists impose restrictions: they require personal initiative, discipline and humility. On the upside, lists allow for autonomy and a sense of security in complex situations. In ritualizing, the list lets people focus on the experience. *Use* the checklist. A checklist only works if it is used.

PLANNING PHASE

 ## QUESTIONNAIRE ON RITUAL IDENTITY

This short questionnaire is designed to help you determine your ritual identity and strategy. Tick off a maximum of ten statements that correspond to your situation: six to eight statements associated with the bold symbols (★, ●, ■, ◆) and two to four of the other symbols (Δ, □).

- ★ I am an active member of a religious institution.
- ● I am an inactive member of a religious institution.
- ■ I am a member of a humanist organization.
- ◆ I belong to a holistic or esoteric group.
- Δ I belong to a religious/secular or humanist group that has no official status.
- □ I consider myself traditional but not religious.
- ★ I attend religious worship services at least once a month.
- ● I attend religious worship services no more than once or twice a year.
- □ I consider myself spiritual but not religious.
- ◆ I belong to a group that celebrates nature or the cosmos.
- Δ I do not feel the need in my life for any religious, civil or philosophical institution or group.
- ■ I can live ethically and fulfil my life based on reason and humanity.

◆ It is important to me to have my wedding/funeral/child's ceremony in a natural setting, if possible in a forest.

☐ I believe humankind must treat the environment and the planet respectfully.

★ I cannot imagine having my wedding/funeral/child's ceremony in a non-religious setting.

● I would love to have my wedding/funeral/child's ceremony in a religious setting but without a priest/pastor/rabbi/other religious leader.

☐ It would be nice to have my wedding/funeral/child's ceremony in a religious setting but without any religious references in the ceremony.

◆ It is important to me to have my wedding/funeral/child's ceremony in a natural setting, far from any man-made structures.

■ I would like to have my wedding/funeral/child's ceremony in a setting that is not religious.

△ I cannot imagine having my wedding/funeral/child's ceremony in a religious setting.

★ I cannot imagine my wedding/funeral/child's ceremony without a priest/pastor/rabbi/other religious leader.

● It does not matter to me whether my wedding/child's ceremony is held in a religious setting, but I cannot imagine a funeral without religious rites.

◆ The planet and its future is in our (human) hands.

★ I want religious texts at my wedding/funeral/child's ceremony.

■ I want my wedding/funeral/child's ceremony to be performed by a humanist celebrant or at least someone with humanist values.

◆ A lifecycle ceremony with a shaman would suit me quite well.

△ I do not need help from any institution (religious, civil or philosophical) to celebrate a lifecycle transition.

● My family/friends expect me to organize a religious wedding/funeral/child's ceremony.

■ I do not need god or any supernatural being in order to live and die well.

☐ I would organize a religious wedding/funeral/child's ceremony not for myself so much as to please/keep peace with my family/friends.

■ My friends/family would find a religious or institutional wedding/funeral/child's ceremony insistent with my personal values.

☐ The religious holidays I celebrate have no significance beyond the fact that they are cultural or social occasions.

Δ I do not need an official leader of any kind to preside over my lifecycle passages, birthdays/wedding, child's ceremony/funeral.

Add up how many times you have ticked each of these six symbols ★, ●, ■, ◆, ☐, Δ. Now turn to the key on page 90 to discover your ritual identity. The key to the questionnaire is found at the end of the chapter.

★ _____

● _____

■ _____

◆ _____

Δ _____

☐ _____

 # FIVE TECHNIQUES FOR FEELING SAFE

We have inherited non-pharmaceutical remedies that can transform our daily lives and help us feel safe. These five exercises represent low-tech corporeal technology that requires no particular conditions, skill or accessories. They can be performed almost anywhere and any time by nearly everyone. In fact, two of the exercises I learned from my son. He was no more than two years old when he started climbing into our bed in the mornings asking for a 'sandwich hug'. Once he had got what he needed, he pushed us apart saying 'go away' and toddled off giggling.

These mind-body-viscera based exercises use our senses, breath, attention shifts and movement to keep us in tune with our basic needs.

HUGGING (USING TOUCH WITH OTHERS)

Do this exercise with a person with whom you feel very comfortable on a physical level. It can calm activation, relieve anxiety and feelings of fear. It is suitable for children and adults. Where there is a great difference in size, such as with small children, the person needing soothing can be held. This exercise is not appropriate in the face of real threat; when activation is called for it will be counter-productive.

- *Positioning:* Stand face to face with your partner with your feet shoulder-width apart and flat on the floor (barefoot or stocking foot is recommended). Place your arms around each other, lean into each other lightly. *Focus on yourself.* Feel your insides quieting down. Let the hug last until you feel still inside (1–3 minutes). An alternative version involves touching foreheads, with or without placing your hands on the other person's shoulders. This version is recommended in contexts where full-length body contact is unacceptable. Rocking has a similar effect and can be done alone (e.g. the rocking in traditional Jewish prayer).

- *For clinicians:* This exercise effectively calms activation. One therapist advises its use to enhance a couple's physical and emotional relationship (Schnarch 1997, pp.157–186).

BUTTERFLY HUG (USING TOUCH ALONE)

The butterfly hug is a self-soothing technique practised alone. It is suitable for anyone who can follow the simple instructions.

- *Positioning:* Turn the palms of your hands towards you and cross your wrists. Interlock your thumbs to form the butterfly's body. Your hands and other fingers are the butterfly wings. Place your thumbs against your upper chest, just below the intersection of the clavicles. (Alternative position: Cross your arms high over your chest and place the tips of your middle fingers lightly on your shoulders, thumbs pointing towards your throat.) Your eyes may be closed, partially closed or even open if you feel safer this way. Turn your eyes inwards towards the tip of your nose.

- *Now you are ready to begin:* Slowly and softly alternate the flapping of your butterfly's wings. Observe your breathing. Bring your breath down into your abdomen. When you feel comfortable with the rhythm of the fluttering, notice any feelings that arise (pleasure, pain, other physical sensations) and what comes up in your mind (thoughts, images, sounds, odours). Observe, but do not judge the feelings or thoughts. Imagine them as fluffy or dark clouds floating high above you. Let a light breeze push them across the sky, beyond your horizon.

- *For clinicians:* The 'butterfly hug' (BH) is a self-administered Bilateral Stimulation (BLS) method (like the eye movement or tapping) to process traumatic material for an individual or for group work. Desensitization (self-soothing) is a reprocessing by-product using the BH as BLS (Artigas and Jarero 1998).

 ## NEAR AND FAR (EYES)

This deceptively simple exercise using the eyes can relieve anxiety and introduce a sense of calm.

- *Positioning:* Place a pencil, a pointer, or use your finger, at arm's length and then draw it towards you until your arm is crooked. Draw your attention and your eyes to the tip of the object or your finger. Now look beyond the tip, along an imaginary line, to the furthest point you can find in the room. Move your eyes back and forth between the points (1–3 minutes). Pause, and then repeat the exercise three times.

- *For clinicians:* This is another exercise I learned from my son. According to David Grand, who calls the exercise 'visual convergence', it activates the oculo-cardiac reflex (OCR), functioning as a primitive, powerful and immediate parasympathetic reflex (vagal manoeuvre), rapidly slowing the heart and calming the body[1] (2013, p.83).

HUMMING (VOICE AND BREATH)

Humming increases energy, stamina and a sense of wellbeing in a surprisingly short time. Even ten minutes of humming can make you feel regenerated. I learned to bring humming to a new level during Dhrupad (an ancient genre of Indian classical music) workshops with Uma Lacombe, during which we hummed or sang for six to seven hours a day. Humming is a marvellous massage of the inner organs!

- *Positioning:* During Uma's workshops we sat in the lotus position, but any upright position is fine. The beneficent effect is as much due to the voice's stimulation of the body as to the changes that occur with rhythmic breathing.

- *For clinicians:* High frequency sounds of about 2000 Hz and higher are stimulating for the brain. Children's voices and most women's voices are high frequency. Other examples include squeaks, a shrill whistle, flute and the higher registers on a violin. Low frequency sounds tire us more easily because we have to block them out to hear the human voice. Low sounds occur at about 500 Hz and lower; some examples of low sounds include: bass drum, tuba, thunder, deep male voice, machines and traffic noise. Humming and singing activate the vagal nerve and correct respiratory, and thus also cardiac and visceral, rhythms (Tomatis 1988, p.63). Singing and playing a wind or brass instrument can produce a similar effect. Short inhalations followed by long exhalations '"gates" the influence of the myelinated vagus on the heart' (Porges 2011, p.254).

---

1   David Grand hypothesizes that people with repeated losses or instability at an early age in their relationship with their primary caretakers (attachment issues) feel calmer when looking close (when the pointer [or pen or finger] is nearby) and more distressed when they are asked to look off into the distance (2013, p.87).

HEAVENLY DRUM (EARS)

Have you ever been so tired that you cannot fall asleep? An evening in a noisy environment can produce the same sensation. Taoists teach an exercise that simultaneously rests and stimulates the inner ear; they call it 'beating the heavenly drum'. (Chang 1986, pp.128–29).

- *Positioning:* Place the index fingers of each hand on the earflaps that allow you to block out sound. Push lightly on the tips of your index fingers until you cut off outside sounds. With the tip of your second finger, tap gently on the finger nails of your index finger. You should hear a metallic sound, similar to the beating of a drum. Tap a slow and regular but steady rhythm (12–36 times). Do three sets of drumming, pausing briefly between each set.

- *For clinicians:* This exercise stimulates and gives rest to the inner ear. On the one hand, the ear needs a rest from hearing sounds that never cease, even when we are asleep. On the other hand, if the inner ear – what Tomatis calls the brain's dynamo (1988) – is too tired, we often have trouble getting to sleep. In 1954, he introduced the concept of a random sonic event or 'electronic gating system' that 'surprises' the muscles of the inner ear; this revitalizes and allows for a restful state (Tomatis 1988, p.127).

 ## PRIORITIZING

This tool helps visualize what is most important to you, whether that be a relationship or a venue. Do this exercise alone if you are at the centre of the ritualization, as a couple, a family or a team if you are crafting the occasion together. It takes about 20 minutes.

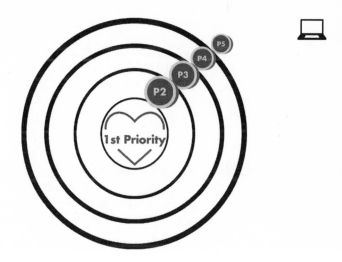

Figure 5.2. How to prioritize
This tool is useful for determining your priorities.

MATERIALS NEEDED

Enlargement of Figure 5.2, writing materials and tracing paper.

FIRST ROUND

This round is about *expectations* – yours and others. Place tracing paper on top of Figure 5.2. Place the names of the people you are *expected* to be close to, or options you think you *should* choose in P1 – this represents your inner circle or first priorities. P2 is your second circle. Place less important people and options in sections P3, P4 and P5. Take a picture of the diagram and label it 'Version A'.

SECOND ROUND

This round is about *feelings*. Identify the people you *feel* close to, or the options that feel right. Take a picture and label it 'Version B'. If this version resembles Version A, you know that you are on the right track. Skip the third round. You are ready to choose who you want to *actively participate* in your ritualization (people from P1, and perhaps from P2). Determine *who will be invited* to participate by their presence (people in P2 and P3, for example). If your versions are quite different, take it to another round.

THIRD ROUND

This round is about *compromise*. Obligations and what we want and need do not always match up. Compare versions A and B. What is it about this person or that choice that makes it difficult for you decide? What creative solutions are there for your situation?

Example 1: Wedding

You have too many guests on your list; you do not know how to handle your mother.

Place yourself and your partner in P1. Your father, a reassuring presence, is in P2. You realize that just the thought of having your mother about as you dress for the wedding makes you nervous; you put your mother in P4. Your funky, upbeat neighbour, a good friend, is in P3. You invent a useful task to honour your mother and ask your friend to help you dress for the wedding. You ask for your father's permission to leave his cousin and his family off the guest list.

Example 2: Funeral

It falls to you to organize your gay uncle's funeral. His partner is with you in P1. Your mother is in P2. A homophobe aunt who never accepted her brother's choices is in P3. You and your uncle's partner ask your mother to speak about her relationship with her brother during the ceremony. The aunt, a photographer, happily makes the programme.

WHO PRESIDES?

As a rule of thumb, *the people at the centre of the ceremony do not preside*. When they do, the result too often resembles a selfie: emotions appear frozen, the shutter-clicker's eyes and attention are focused elsewhere, the sense of the event is lost. Consequently, the feelings generated cannot be genuinely supported. Newly-weds should feel free to concentrate on each other as they pronounce their wedding vow. A retiree should not have to open the festivities in his honour. The presider has a supporting role, like that of a midwife[2] (see Figure 4.2). The midwife accompanies and assists a mother as she goes into labour and brings her child into the world. Whether the person who presides at the ceremony is a professional or an amateur, the objective is to ensure that the ceremony proceeds as planned and that those at the centre are shown to best advantage.

DO YOU NEED A PROFESSIONAL?

Hiring a professional celebrant is recommended for weddings and funerals. In the case of less formal events, the accompaniment of a professional can be constructive in the planning and creating phases, but maybe superfluous in the realizing phase. A friend or family member is often the best choice to preside here. Out of respect for this person, the content must be complete and the format clear.

Professional support is indicated if:

- you are seriously ill, newly unemployed or facing a crisis

- you face family resistance to your plan for a secular ceremony

- you suspect that your values or vision of the future are incompatible with those of the other craftspeople on the team

- your or your partner's ritual identity is Institutional or Distanced.

BASIC TIPS

- Do your homework. Decide exactly what you need and what you want the presider to do: accompany, conduct the ceremony, or both (see Table 5.1). Be wary of anyone who might steal the show.

- If you decide to hire a professional, check their professional training, accreditation and celebrant's network. Clear up as many questions as possible by telephone or email. Interview only celebrants who fit your basic criteria (first impression, professionalism, availability).

2   The term 'midwife' is composed of 'mid', an obsolete Middle English preposition meaning 'with', and 'wif' or woman. In French, a midwife is known as a *sage femme*, which means 'wise woman'.

Fees vary greatly from region to region. As with most services, the least expensive is not always the best choice. Professionals who craft bespoke ceremonies must charge higher rates; typically they invest 20–40 hours in crafting a ceremony.

- Trust your instincts!

Presiding is a service role. The person you choose to preside at your ceremony must be able to put the focus on you and your objectives for the ritualization, provide timely advice and support you unconditionally on this special occasion.

TABLE 5.1. WHAT DOES PRESIDING INVOLVE?

	PROFESSIONAL CELEBRANT	AMATEUR ARTISAN	PERSON AT CENTRE
GOAL	To accompany *others* as they ritualize a transition or event	To ritualize a transition or event for a *loved one* (e.g. funeral)	To ritualize a transition or event for *oneself* (e.g. separation, loss)
REQUIREMENTS	Training + ability to accompany Experience in speaking in public Sensitivity and respect for the values of the person at the centre *Calm presence* *Selfless service* (others' desires, needs, interests come first) Maintains emotional *distance* *Asks:* What does this event mean to you? Assumes *supporting role*	No training necessary Authenticity Respect for the values of the person at the centre *Calm presence* Disciplined approach Ability to look after *own* needs as well as the interests of the person in *central* role Exploration of *other's feelings* *Asks oneself:* What does this event mean to him/her/us? Assumes a visible but *secondary* role	No training necessary Authenticity Consciousness of one's own values *Involved presence* Disciplined approach Looks after *own* desires, needs, interests Exploration of *own feelings* *Asks oneself:* What does this event mean to me/us? Assumes the *central* role

CREATING PHASE

WHY AND HOW?

This exercise facilitates brainstorming about why you are ritualizing this occasion and how you imagine the ceremony. It should take no more than 15 minutes.

MATERIALS NEEDED
A sheet of paper and writing tools for each person, plus one extra sheet for the group discussion.

QUESTIONS
Craftspeople work separately on the questions below. Note down the answers that come readily. Follow your gut feelings.

- *Why* is this occasion important to me?
  - What do I want to convey? (Keep it down to 3–5 words, e.g. wedding: our love for each other; funeral: my respect for my father; naming ceremony: our commitment to our son.)

- *How* do I envisage the ceremony?
  - *What* do I NOT want to see, hear or do?

If you are working alone, you may want to check your answers with a good friend, therapist, celebrant or coach. You can now move on to the next tasks in this phase.

As a crafting team, share your ideas about Why and How. Set aside judgement and listen to each person's ideas. Now ask: What do we want to convey as a group through this ceremony? Identify (1) which aspects are clear to all and (2) where negotiation is needed. Have we taken into account the group discussions and needs of different members of the group? Tackle the areas that need to be negotiated and make a final version. Once you have agreement on what you want to convey, you have finished the exercise and can move on to the next tasks.

CORE VALUES

This exercise looks at how values evolve over time. It is geared towards those at the centre of the ceremony. If you are working on a funeral, concentrate on the deceased and the values that characterized his or her life. (Suggestions for terms are found in Table 5.2.)

PAST: VALUES I (WE) GREW UP WITH

- What was I taught to value?

- What was I taught about the importance of
  - achievement/success
  - work at school/job
  - money/power
  - relationships with others
  - appearance
  - independence
  - hobbies, sports and other free-time activities
  - sexuality
  - religion/spiritual practice
  - nature/the environment.

PRESENT: VALUES I (WE) HAVE KEPT

- Which of the above values have I discarded or adapted to my life today?

- Which values have I retained?

- What set of core values are important to me now?

FUTURE: VALUES TO GUIDE ME (US)

- Which of the core values identified above (past and present) do I see guiding me into the future? Concretely, how do I see them being transmitted or put into practice?

At the end of the exercise, boil your list of values down to *three to five words or short phrases*. Now you are ready to see how these concepts can be used in your ceremony.

PLUMBING THE MEANING OF CORE VALUES

Take the words or phrases that represent core values. Let's say you chose these three words: *beauty – generosity – security*. You now have what you need to compose:

- Promise and accompanying texts (new arrival or wedding ceremony)
- Guidelines for life (coming of age event)
- Assessment (retirement, menopause, anniversary)
- Homage (funeral)
- Opening address (social or civic event).

Surprisingly, the three values identified above may be appropriate in all of these contexts. What they mean must be developed, because it depends on the context and the people concerned. While one person may see beauty as an aesthetic sense, another may think only of physical attractiveness. Generosity can bring up a rich feeling of giving for some and evoke receiving for others. Security may mean money in the bank or strong locks on windows and doors.

If you are crafting a wedding, these three core values express what love and marriage mean to you as a couple. They form the base of your vows, the texts you write, the music you choose and the gestures you perform. These same three words used at a funeral represent the values of the deceased. They might also be the theme of a conference or public event. As in the case of a graduation ceremony, the meaning attributed to these values will depend on the speaker's perspective as a student, teacher, parent or school administrator.

Imagine a circumstance or time when this core value has been put to the test and another in which it is fully expressed. Turn this into a vignette or a short description that reveals concretely how this value is or was put into practice in your life, relationship or by the deceased. If possible, let your text sit for a few hours, days or even weeks. Come back to it now and again to ask: Does this fit? Does it feel right? Authenticity and coherence are of the essence.

The 'values' (words) in the following table are to be used with both the *Core values* tool and the *Plumbing the meaning* tool.

TABLE 5.2. TERMS EXPRESSING CORE VALUES

Accepting	Accommodating	Adventurous	Affectionate
Agreeable	Allegiance	Alluring	Altruistic
Ambitious	Analytical	Appreciative	Articulate
Artistic	Assertive	Attentive	Authentic
Balanced	Beauty	Broad-minded	Calm
Candid	Careful	Cheerful	Clever
Comforting	Commitment	Communicative	Compassionate
Competent	Conscientious	Cooperative	Courageous
Creative	Curiosity	Decisive	Dependable
Devoted	Dignity	Diplomatic	Discreet
Easy-going	Educated	Effective	Efficient
Elegance	Empathy	Encouraging	Entertaining
Enthusiastic	Excellence	Exploration	Fairness
Family	Fidelity	Flexibility	Forgiving
Forthright	Freedom	Friendship	Frugal
Gracious	Grateful	Generous	Genuine
Good sport	Good-tempered	Happiness	Hard-working
Harmony	Helpful	Honest	Honourable
Hopeful	Humane	Humble	Humorous
Imaginative	Industrious	Inquisitive	Insightful
Integrity	Intelligence	Intuitive	Joy
Justice	Kindness	Knowledge	Leadership
Love	Loyalty	Maturity	Mindfulness

Modesty	Motivation	Obedience	Open-mindedness
Openness	Optimism	Order	Originality
Passion	Peace	Perceptive	Perfection
Piety	Pleasant	Pleasure	Polite
Power	Practicalness	Pragmatism	Precision
Professionalism	Purity	Quick-witted	Realism
Relaxation	Reliability	Resourceful	Respectful
Security	Self-control	Self-discipline	Selflessness
Serenity	Service	Sharing	Simplicity
Sincerity	Skilfulness	Sociable	Solidarity
Spirited	Spirituality	Stability	Strength
Support	Sympathy	Tactful	Talented
Teamwork	Thoughtful	Tidy	Tolerant
Truthful	Trust	Understanding	Unity
Valour	Well-mannered	Well-spoken	Wisdom

 ## MAPPING IT OUT

Before walking out the door in search of adventure, you need to know what direction to take, if only to find a means of transport and to get there on time. This tool is specially designed for ritualizing Coming of Age. You may also find it useful in the preparation of other occasions such as a birthday celebration or a retirement party.

Now that you have a few key words or phrases that represent your core values, explore what is at the heart of this transition for you and discuss it.

- Why is it important for *me* to mark this transition into adulthood? What difference will it make to *me*?

- What do *I* expect to happen or hope to accomplish by marking this passage?

- How will *I* know that my goals have been reached?

- Might it change how others see me? If so, how?

This part of the exercise is concerned with What, When, Where and How.

First step: What activities do I enjoy doing?

Second step: Which of these activities are done alone, which in a group?

Third step: Which of these could I imagine doing for my coming of age event? Measure your ideas against these questions:

- How is it related to my core values? Does it help me live out or reinforce my values?

- How does this plan bring me a step closer to adulthood? Do I have support for it?

- What do I need to organize it?

Whatever you decide to do, make sure you feel both supported and that it has the potential to anchor you and your family in a new reality.

If you had a clear idea from the start of how you want to ritualize this passage, it is hoped that this process has confirmed your desire for your project. If you had no clue about what to do, perhaps you know now how to proceed. You should feel free to put the decision off until later.

COHERENCE TEST

Once you have clarified your core values, you are ready to *finalize the choices made in the planning phase* about Who, What, When and Where. Use the *Coherence test* to ensure that the ceremony is consistent with your values and harmonious with the event as a whole. Do the choices you made in the planning phase regarding kind of ceremony, people, venue, date and time still fit? Are they coherent with the values of the person or event at the centre of the ceremony? Note your values in the first column in Table 5.3 below. Run through the ceremony and identify where and how these values are expressed.

TABLE 5.3. COHERENCE GRID

CAN I (WE) STATE IT? *LIST CORE VALUES BELOW*	DO I (WE) EXPRESS IT?	HOW IS THE VALUE EXPRESSED IN OUR CHOICES ABOUT WHO, WHAT, WHEN WHERE, HOW OR WHY?

JUST THE RIGHT MUSIC

Music can set the mood and enhance meaning in a ceremony. It may also serve as a 'breather' after an intensely emotional moment. Music for entrances and exits must be long enough for people to move from one spot to another. Pieces used during the ceremony should be short. Two to three minutes can seem very long to a couple eager to pronounce their vows, to young children and to mourners. If you plan to add music, choose pieces that fit your goals, your core values and the meaning the occasion has for you.

- A reminder of a particular moment in your life together (*wedding ceremony*)

- A song that makes your child's eyes light up (*new arrival ceremony*)

- A favourite singer or band (*coming of age event*)

- Something that corresponds to this phase of life (*retirement, menopause, anniversary*)

- The deceased's preferred music or a piece that reminds friends and family of the deceased (*funeral*)

- Traditional pieces of music judged appropriate for the occasion (*social or civic event*)

How many pieces do you need? Is the music recorded or will it be played by amateur or professional musicians? How long or short should the pieces be? Where do they fit in the ceremony? Who is responsible for the music on the day of the ceremony? Who is responsible for putting it on at the right time or for cueing the musicians?

 ## SMALL GESTURES, BIG IMPACT

Every culture uses gestures and symbols to mark important occasions. Sharing food and drink (social gathering) and exchanging property (wedding rings) are widely understood and considered fitting for secular ritualization. Other gestures, such as the act of sprinkling water on a child (baptism) or on a coffin (funeral), are too closely tied to religious rites to be used with impunity in secular settings. Be wary, too, of misappropriating rituals from other cultures.

Be curious. Investigate the gestures and symbols of your cultural tradition(s) or origin. Ask older relatives how they and their parents celebrated the major events in their own lives (wedding, welcoming a child, funeral). When did your grandmother *feel* married? What do you need to do to feel like you have made the transition? Maybe you do not want to stomp on a glass at the end of your wedding ceremony, but it inspires you to do something else that ties in with your core values. Ask yourselves what you want the gesture or symbol to express:

- Appreciation for our parents? Our union? Our future together? (*wedding ceremony*)

- Our desire for support as we face this new phase in our family's life? (*new arrival ceremony*)

- Recognition of our child as adult? (*parents*) I'm ready to test my wings! (*child*) (*coming of age event*)

- What symbolizes this new phase in my life? (*retirement, menopause, anniversary*)

- What do I feel I need to do to let you go? (*funeral*)

- What are the symbols of this event? How should we use them to transmit our values? (*social or civic event*)

Simple, intentional acts are poignant.

- Shaking hands with newly-weds and their parents (*wedding ceremony*)

- Demonstrating your blessing of a new arrival by touching the baby's foot, hand or head (*new arrival ceremony*)

- Gifting your child with the great-aunt's painting he long admired (*coming of age event*)

- Using that beloved but chipped teacup as a symbol of a new phase in life (*retirement, menopause, anniversary*)

- Placing a hand on the casket before it is buried (*funeral*)

- Writing a note with your best wishes or sympathy in a guest book (*funeral, wedding, naming ceremony, social or civic event*)

 FORMAT OF THE CEREMONY

The format of your ceremony is the framework that holds it together. Depending on the context, your format may be a simple list (naming ceremony) or an elaborate schema (wedding ceremony, civic event). All of the craftspeople should participate in the three rounds described below.

Order of a sample ceremony

BEGINNING

- *Music* – arrival in ceremonial space
- *Welcome* – presider

MIDDLE

- *Speaker* – close relative
- *Speaker* – friend
- *Music*
- *Heart of the ceremony*
- *Symbolic gesture*

END

- *Words of closure* – presider
- *Music* – departure from ceremonial space
- *Social gathering*

FIRST ROUND

Imagine who will do what and what will happen when, and what it will look like in the venue you have chosen. Play the 'film' in your head. Share and compare these ideas with your 'team'.

SECOND ROUND

(1) Write up a simple order of events (see the Order of a sample ceremony box) and then adapt it to meet your needs. (2) Alternate lighter and more serious contributions. Always prepare an introduction to each contribution and present the person who reads it. (3) Make a drawing of the setting and mark out your ideal choreography. As you move through each aspect of the event, keep your core values in mind and check for coherence at each step. (4) Include a seating plan.

THIRD ROUND

Visit the venue with the craftspeople, if possible at the same hour of the day as the ceremony. With your 'Order of ceremony' in hand, walk it through to see if it works for you. Ask yourself: Do I feel comfortable standing here? Can I imagine standing or sitting here with family and friends in front of me? Do I feel all right having them that close/far away? Can I see the presider, musicians, speakers? Do I feel comfortable with the choreography as a whole? If not, what can I change so as to feel more at ease?

FINALIZE THE ORDER OF THE CEREMONY

Make a list of the items you will need at the venue on the day of the ceremony. Note who is responsible for bringing each one of them and for putting them into place.

REALIZING PHASE

RITUALIZING, STEP BY STEP

PREPARING THE SETTING

Setting up usually begins about two hours before the start of the ceremony. The sound system team, decorators, florists and caterers should be in place and ready at least an hour before the arrival of the guests. Depending on local customs and cultural expectations, this may mean one hour or fifteen minutes before the announced time.

At this point, the people actively involved in the ceremony (presider, craftspeople, greeters, participants, musicians) are present. Those using a microphone should test it. If the reception area is within earshot of the ceremonial space, the caterers must keep quiet or take a break during the ceremony; they must be ready to serve, however, the minute it is over.

OPENING AND CARRYING THE EVENT

When the presider indicates it is time to begin, the greeters show the guests to their seats. A change in the music – or a short silence if music is already being played – signals an entrance or a transition in the ceremony. The presider also deals with unexpected events such as late arrivals, crying children, noise from passing vehicles or a person who is unwell. This may mean modifying the procedure, shifting everyone's attention or, on the contrary, simply stating what is happening.

TRANSITIONING FROM CEREMONY TO SOCIALIZING

The presider should preserve a solemn tone as he or she closes the ceremony. Explanations about when and how to leave the ceremonial space are given only if they are absolutely necessary. The organizer ensures that people can move smoothly from the formal ceremonial space to where the social gathering is held.

CLOSING THE EVENT

At the end of the event, the organizer is attentive to people's needs as they make ready to leave, and he or she assumes responsibility for or supervises the clean-up.

GUIDELINES FOR READERS

Readers should arrive prepared for public speaking (appearance, text and voice). In an emotional situation, arrange for a backup person to accompany you to the lectern.

- Your role is important but secondary to the occasion.

- If you are reading a text of your own composition, submit it well in advance to those crafting the ritual.

- Practise reading aloud.

- Stand rather than sit: it is easier to feel present and remain attentive to your feelings.

- Test your voice – with the microphone – well before people arrive. When using a handheld microphone, press it lightly against your chin and hold it there throughout the reading; it will follow your movements and project your voice evenly.

- Walk up to the lectern at a natural pace. Exhale. Place your feet slightly apart. Do not lock your knees.

- Keep hand and facial gestures to a minimum. Link your hands behind your back or let them fall comfortably at your side; keep them out of your pockets. Try not to grip or lean over the lectern.

- If emotions do well up, let them. Pause. Take a breath. Drink some water. If you feel you cannot carry on, move to the side the lectern, and signal to your backup person to take over.

PREPARING YOUR FUNERAL

A living will concerns three areas: body, belongings and being. Forms can be obtained from notary publics, lawyers, at most hospitals and on many funeral home websites. It is an act of love and respect for loved ones to put in writing what you want to happen and who should be named responsible if you should become unable to decide about your health treatment and property (and debts). You know best what kind of funeral would be most appropriate. The contents of this exercise may be attached to your living will.

- In one or two sentences explain *your vision of your life*. 'I see my life as...'

- Write *a brief biography* with the important events and dates in chronological order with either succinct prose or bullet point format. It may be easier to write in the third person ('he or she was born...').

- If you write an *obituary announcement* ensure that it is respectful of your family and relationships. Do not use it to unilaterally prune the family tree and settle disputes.

- Make a list of *people who should be notified* individually on your death. Include full names and up-to-date contact information.

- Appoint one or two *people responsible* for the implementation of the funeral.

- *Questions:* What kind of funeral would be coherent with your values and life? What would you not want in your funeral? What place might you suggest for the ceremony? Do you want burial or cremation? If you have special wishes, check their legality in your area.

KEY TO QUESTIONNAIRE
ON RITUAL IDENTITY

- ★ (5*) *Institutional.* If this symbol ★ represents the majority of your answers, your religious practice is regular and satisfying. Religious ceremony is important and coherent with your values and view of life. You marked these symbols Δ, □ no more than three times.

- ● (5) *Distanced.* If you ticked a majority of this symbol ● you feel distant ties with a religious institution; you practise occasionally. Ceremonies held in this setting may or may not satisfy your need to mark a transition. You may have also marked the symbol ★ once or twice but these symbols Δ, □ no more than three times.

- ■ (6) *Secular/Humanist.* A majority of this symbol ■ indicates that you are indifferent or against religion. You do not identify yourself with traditional religious circles. You need tailor-made ceremonies to mark life events. You may be a member of a humanist or secular group. You marked these symbols Δ, □ a number of times.

- ◆ (5) *Alternative.* If you marked this symbol at least three times you probably find yourself most comfortable with a holistic approach to life and may be a member of an esoteric group. Bespoke ceremonies suit you well; you may not feel the need for a celebrant or any kind of authority figure to ritualize.

- Δ (5) *Unaffiliated.* You do not associate yourself with any institution and are likely to be critical of institutions in general. You may belong to groups with little official status and feel uncomfortable in institutional settings. It is important you feel free to craft the kind of rituals that are right for you.

- □ (7) *Traditional.* Traditional cultural or social activities are important to your sense of identity. You will want traditional words and gestures in your bespoke ceremony.

Note: * = maximum number.

CRAFTING MEANINGFUL RITUAL

Whereas Part II lays down the basics for ritualizing, the chapters in Part III adapt the approach to specific situations. Each chapter is preceded by a checklist that is divided into the three phases presented in Part II: *Planning*, *Creating* and *Realizing*. The checklists accompany the creative process; they do not explain how to ritualize. The *Creating* phase is the secret to the craft of meaningful ritual.

CHECKLIST FOR A NAMING CEREMONY

PLANNING
First things first

☐ We are clear about our objectives for this ceremony

We have identified:
☐ **About whom?** The newcomer
☐ **By whom?** Parents are responsible for **crafting/ organizing/presiding**
☐ **With whom?** who **participates/is invited** (godparents, grandparents, siblings)
☐ **What kind of event?**
☐ **When?** A fitting **date/time** for the event
☐ **Where?** A suitable **place/setting/venue**

COMMUNICATION AND CONTINGENCY
☐ We have contacted or invited all ('With whom?') noted above
☐ Participants have approved their roles
☐ If there is disagreement about how to proceed we know who makes the final decision
☐ We have contingency plans for 'Where?' and leeway for timing

PAUSE

CREATING
Making sense (parents)

We, the craftspeople, are agreed on:
☐ **Why and how** we are ritualizing the arrival of our child
☐ What is at the **HEART ♥** of this ceremony
☐ The **key values, ideals or philosophy of life** we wish to transmit to our child
☐ **Decisions confirmed** (Who, What, When, Where)
☐ If there is disagreement, we have discussed the issues

CONTENT
☐ **Words ♥ Promises** parents, godparents, others
☐ **Music**
☐ **Gestures/symbols/objects**

FORMAT
☐ **ENTRY** INTO CEREMONIAL SPACE
☐ **Welcome**
☐ **Heart ♥ Promises** to our child
☐ **Closing/exit** ceremonial space > transition
☐ **Social gathering**
☐ **Choreography/scenography** check for visual participation
☐ **Reminder list**
☐ **We have checked for flow and choreography**

PAUSE

REALIZING
Expressing meaning

☐ **Prepare setting** (parents/presider/organizer)

☐ **Open ceremony** (presider/parents)
☐ **Ritualizing** (Content + Format)
  ♦ Conduct (presider) ♦ Participate (all)
☐ **Close ceremony** (presider)

☐ **Open social part of event** (organizer)
☐ **Social gathering** (all)
☐ **Close event and clean up** (parents/organizer)

DURATION OF EVENT (suggested)
Ceremony (5–15 minutes)
Social gathering (2–4 hours)

April 2016. This checklist is not intended to be comprehensive. Modifications to fit specific situations are encouraged.

ASHØKA®

6

BIRTH AND BEGINNINGS

Regardless of race, colour religion, sex and
nationality, every child has the right to:

- healthy mental and physical development

- a name and nationality

- sufficient food, housing and medical care

- free education, play and recreation

- immediate aid in the event of disasters and emergencies

- protection from cruelty, neglect and exploitation

- protection from persecution and to an upbringing in
  the spirit of (sisterhood), brotherhood and peace.

*The 'Declaration of the Rights of a Child' was adopted unanimously
on 20 November 1959 by the General Assembly of the United Nations.*

The arrival of a child into the world can be a magical and unforgettable
experience. The African adage, 'it takes a village to raise a child' is a
reminder that childrearing is not done in isolation. Few families still
live in real villages or even in tightly-knit communities, so parents today
are definitely out there on the frontline. There is much talk today about
children's rights and the conditions noted above are indeed important

in creating a healthy social and physical environment for children. However, they do not guarantee happiness. Children who lack some of these basic conditions may be better off than privileged children who – to all appearances – have them all. In order to thrive, children need to feel safe. This means having at least one adult caregiver who cares for them by holding them, looking them in the eyes, talking to them and playing with them. For this reason alone, a welcoming ceremony is in order, because it gives parents an excellent opportunity to reach out to the people in their 'village'. All parents have expectations about the roles they want their family and friends to take. On their side, grandparents, godparents or sponsors, uncles, aunts, brothers, sisters, cousins and friends may also have ideas about the kind of relationship they want to have with the child. Their contributions to the child's welfare are more likely to match the parents' expectations if they are spelled out clearly early on. The ceremony offers a fitting framework for the parents and their guests to express and manage these expectations.

Welcoming ceremonies should be happy occasions, and they usually are. Yet, as parents are faced with the fragility of life and many new challenges, brothers and sisters may, or may not, see the new arrival as a bundle of joy. All newcomers have special needs. The birth may have been difficult, the adoption fraught with complications. Perhaps the child's legal or social status prevents him or her from being fully integrated into a new family. Regardless of the circumstances, every child needs to feel safe and cherished.

A secular celebration that marks the arrival of a child – or even an adolescent or an adult – into a family or a new community can be simple or elaborate. In either case, it serves two functions. First of all, the newcomer is publicly received into the group. Second, the group implicitly or explicitly acknowledges its responsibilities for the new person. Sometimes referred to as a 'naming ceremony', this event is usually rather short and informal. A social gathering – often in the form of a shared meal – nearly always follows.

The main ingredients of a meaningful ceremony include promises, symbolic gestures and music that are coherent with the values the parents want to transmit to their child. A short original pledge that comes from the godmother's heart will be remembered much longer than a beautiful poem by a famous author, especially if her commitment includes regular babysitting – and she follows through on it! A brilliant rendition of a Bach fugue may please the adults, but launching the ceremony with a song that makes the children's eyes light up will get everyone's attention.

Figure 6.1. New arrivals
A young child is in his or her parents' care. Grandparents, godparents, family members and friends show their support for the parents and their child during the ceremony.

SIX SITUATIONS

COLIN

Colin's family loves birds. They have an aviary in their garden and organize their holidays around visits to sanctuaries for migratory birds. Colin's parents asked their guests in advance to prepare a wish for their child. His parents began the ceremony by welcoming everyone and naming their child.

We decided to call our child Colin Andrew + *Family Name*. We welcome him into our lives and ask you to welcome him too.

We chose the name Colin because in many languages it means 'victory of the people'. We see his coming into the world as a victory. Colin was born shortly after the death of his grandfather Andrew. His grandfather lives on for us in Colin's second name.

COLIN'S PARENTS' PROMISE

Colin Andrew, we are overjoyed to be able to *share* our lives with you. We promise you our *love* and *support* through every phase of your life. We promise to teach you how to develop your skills in *friendship* and *empathy* as well as a *sense of justice*.

COLIN'S GODMOTHER KOKO'S PROMISE

Colin, like you, I love birds. My name is a bird's name in Japanese. An ancient legend from my country promises that anyone who folds a thousand origami cranes will be granted a wish. I folded 1000 cranes; my wish is for your happiness. I promise to help you discover the secret of a happy life. Being happy implies not just living, but learning how to make your life happy.

Each guest wrote their promise in Colin's guestbook and then on a sheet of paper they folded into an origami bird. The parents helped their children hang their bird-shaped promises on a tree in the family's garden.

LUCY

A priest baptized Manu and Elena's first two children. For many reasons, the parents felt that a baptism was not appropriate for their third child. They called on me to help them organize a non-religious celebration at their home. A short informal ceremony with no religious symbols apart from the elder children's christening candles was held in the presence of a close circle of family and friends. Manu and Elena's promise to their daughter was followed by Lucy's siblings and godfather's promises.

PARENTS' PROMISE

Lucy

We promise to *love* you without clinging to you.

We promise to encourage your *confidence in yourself* while keeping our fears to ourselves.

We promise to *share* the best of *our two cultures* with you by teaching you to how to celebrate their festivals and to respect the principles unique to each one.

SISTER'S PROMISE

Lucy, I promise always to help you and play with you.

BROTHER'S PROMISE

I promise to teach Lucy to play football.

GODFATHER'S PROMISE

Lucy, I will be there for you and help you learn to live life fully by appreciating each one of your six senses.

Through sight, I will help you see the magic in life.

Through hearing, I will help you listen to silence.

Through smell, I will help you identify the scents of nature.

Through taste, I will help you develop your taste for life.

Through touch, I will help you feel what is in your heart.

Through intuition, I will help you sort out what is good for you.

Manu then picked up a flower pot that had been painted by the older children. He placed it on a low table, so that even the youngest guest could see it. A bit of earth from the Portuguese village where he grew up was poured into the pot. Elena added some sandy soil from her hometown in Slovenia. Together the family planted herbs in the pot.

> Every time we look at this brightly coloured pot, we will be reminded of our commitment to you, Lucy. When the plants die, we will replace them with others. Our love for you will never die!

SAMUEL

Pablo is Swiss, born in Argentina to a Protestant pastor. But he is an atheist. Rebecca was raised in Australia by secular Jewish parents. But she discovered spirituality in India.

When their son Samuel was born, Pablo and Rebecca decided to teach him their different roots, traditions and philosophies and trust him to find his own path. With Protestantism, Hinduism and atheism, it seemed easy. But Judaism was more challenging.

Men don't feel Jewish if they are not circumcised. The operation is carried out by a *mohel* on the eighth day after birth. The rite marks a boy's entry into the community. Samuel's parents could have let him decide later on, but the operation is painful for a teenager or an adult. They wanted him to choose his path without going through any trauma. So they decided to proceed with the circumcision…in order to set him free.

Still, Pablo and Rebecca were concerned that the Jewish ritual, which leaves a permanent symbol, would trump their message. So they imagined a relatively simple solution. They chose a suitable date and organized the circumcision in the morning, inviting only close relatives and keeping the event very low-key. In the afternoon, they had a secular naming ceremony during a big reception with extended family and many friends.

Pablo and Rebecca thanked everybody for coming and explained how important it was to them that their son would grow up feeling comfortable in their different cultures. The baby's parents, sisters and godparents read personal commitments that they had written in a guestbook. Pablo then asked the guests to write their own messages to Samuel, conveying what they hoped to teach, transmit or be for him in the years to come. A basketful of stickers made it easy to illustrate their commitment in a playful way.

Every year on Samuel's birthday, the guestbook reminds them of this secular ceremony, the rite they value most.

COSIMA

Cosima's severe disabilities meant many adjustments for her family. When her condition stabilized, her parents decided it was time to properly welcome Cosima into the family. They also wanted to show their gratitude to those who regularly lent them support. On her fifth birthday, Cosima's parents organized a joyful celebration. They adapted and read a text inspired by a Jewish prayer.

> We waited so impatiently for our beautiful Cosima;
> we could not imagine what living with her would be like.
> One should first see the light side of a child,
> and the shadow side later.
> Why did we have to see her pain-filled suffering face first?
>
> So much grief, worry and agony!
> Many mornings our sheets were cold with sweat and tears.
> The whys still haunt our sleep at times.
> How much we rely on you, our friends and families.
> We need your support because we do not have the courage
> every day to face this ordeal alone.
>
> Our dearest Cosima, long before you were born
> we promised to love you, no matter what.
> Your winsome charm and fragility demands the best from each
> one of us.
> There is no doubt that we all have much
> to learn together.

They then asked their guests to playfully assume the role of good fairies. Cosima laughed excitedly as each guest waved their 'magic wand' over her head, blessed her with sweet wishes and then surrounded her with brightly wrapped gifts. They all made drawings for her and pasted them into a book small enough to accompany Cosima whenever she went to hospital.

APINYA

Apinya was born and adopted in Thailand by a Canadian couple. When she was two years old, her parents sought out a Thai Buddhist monk and told him of their desire for a welcoming ceremony for their daughter. After consulting an astrological calendar, the monk suggested the couple come to the temple the following Friday at 9am for a ceremony with their families and friends. The parents welcomed their guests by telling Apinya's story.

> When we first met our daughter, she already had a first name, Apinya, which means 'magical power'. As you can all see, she does indeed have magical powers over us! At the adoption ceremony we choose to add a second name, Karin, because it gives her the choice of a name that maybe easier to use in our culture. Today, her name is Apinya Karin + *Family Name.*

After a short blessing by the monk, Apinya's sponsor, a practitioner of Buddhism, made her this promise: 'A child needs to be fed spiritually from a young age. I intend to help Apinya learn kindness, patience, honesty, compassion and wisdom'. The monk and the sponsor presented her with a certificate. At the end of the ceremony, Apinya's family and friends gathered for a convivial time with music, food and drinks in the temple.

EDWARD

Edward's parents asked their own parents to make a family tree with their respective lineages. At the beginning of Edward's naming ceremony his parents read this text:

Our child, we promise to...
raise you with love
transmit to you what we hold dearest in life
help you become yourself
help you discover your own unique spirit
support you without hanging on to you
celebrate each of the major events of your life with you
support you in what you decide to undertake
teach you the power of pardon
help you see that happiness is not tied to circumstances
share with you the myths and history of our culture...

Adapted from Mallika Chopra's book 100 Promises for My Child

Then they explained that the child had a grandfather on one side and a great-grandfather on the other side with this same name.

GRANDPARENTS' PROMISE

Dear Edward, we had the pleasure of being parents to your parents. Now we are happy to see you, their children, come into the world.

May you grow up harmoniously within our family, surrounded by our love and the love of friends and so, step by step, become who you are meant to be!

The grandparents then added Edward's name and picture to the family tree. His father invited each family member to paste their own picture next to their name. He added: 'It is our hope that knowing where he fits in will help Edward to take his rightful place in our family.' At the end of the ceremony, the cousins decorated the edges of the page.

CHECKLIST FOR A NAMING CEREMONY

The checklist in this chapter is designed to keep you, the child's parents, on course as you craft a meaningful ceremony to welcome your child. The tools listed below are found in Chapter 5.

Set aside 30 minutes for the Planning phase and about two to three hours for the Creating phase. The Realizing phase is broken down into three parts: preparation time (variable), ceremony (five to 15 minutes) and social gathering (two to four hours). Remember that the attention span of children under five years old is limited.

PLANNING PHASE

You will finalize your choices for Who, When and Where during the Creating phase.

 The *Questionnaire on ritual identity* is essential for parents who do not share the same personal, religions or cultural values. Consider hiring a professional celebrant, if you are not on the same page.

 Use *Prioritizing* to determine who to invite.

Use *Who presides?* In most cases, one of the parents, a relative or a friend can preside.

Who?
The event is above all about your child. You – the newcomer's parents – are in second position (see Figure 6.1).

When?
Choose a date and time that suits you and your loved ones best.

Where?
Take the needs of your guests into account, including accessibility for the elderly and safety for small children as well as meal and nap times.

Does the venue have areas that might be dangerous for children? If so, how will you handle this risk?

PAUSE

CREATING PHASE

Creating is fun, but it also involves work. In this phase you will identify your common values and your goals for your child's future, then put your thoughts and dreams into words, gestures and music.

Why?

What does it mean to us to be the parents of this child? What are our hopes and dreams for our child? What are our fears for her/his future? Does her/his arrival represent any obstacles to our family's happiness? What are we willing to invest or give up to achieve these goals?

Why and how? provides a framework for addressing these important questions: Why is it important for us to celebrate this occasion?

How?

How do you envisage the ceremony? In most cases, public commitment to the child and parents is at the heart of the celebration.

Core values explores your shared values and helps you identify a few key words that represent the theme of the ceremony.

The *Coherence test* helps confirm the choices you made in the planning phase.

Content

The elements assembled during the Creating phase make up the content of the ceremony.

Plumbing the meaning of core values applies your core values to the writing of your joint promise and short texts or phrases that communicate in a concrete manner what you mean by these values. Try to make a first draft before taking a look at what others wrote for their welcoming ceremony.

- How do we want to pass on our values to our child?

- What kind of support do we need from our 'village'?

 Just the right music. Use music to gather everyone together and to accompany you as you move towards the social gathering.

 Small gestures, big impact explores how to choose objects and gestures that help visualize your core values. The situations above show how some families used ordinary objects in their child's ceremony.

Format

The ceremonial part kicks off the event. It clarifies the parent's intention and unites people in their purpose.

 Format of the ceremony. Feeling at ease in an informal setting requires good choreography. Walk the ceremony through several times – preferably in the space you have chosen for the ceremony – to make sure that what you have in mind works and will be immediately obvious to your guests.

PAUSE

REALIZING PHASE

These two tools help parents and participants prepare to ritualize the child's ceremony:

Ritualizing step by step. See the tool in Chapter 5.

Guidelines for readers. See the tool in Chapter 5.

RISK FACTORS FOR THE CEREMONY

Crafting a tailor-made ceremony requires the cooperation and investment of both parents. The main risk is losing sight of the newcomer.

CHECKLIST FOR RITUALIZING COMING OF AGE

PLANNING
First things first

☐ We are clear about our objectives for this event

We have identified:

☐ **About whom?** 1) Youth 2) Family
☐ **By whom?** Young person + trusted adult are responsible for **crafting and organizing**
☐ **With whom?** Who **participates** and who is **invited?** (godparents, friends)

COMMUNICATION AND CONTINGENCY
☐ We have contacted or invited all ('With whom?') noted above
☐ Participants have approved their roles
☐ If there is disagreement about how to proceed we know who makes the final decision
☐ We have contingency plans and leeway for timing

PAUSE

CREATING
Making sense (youth + adult)

We, the craftspeople, are agreed on:

☐ **Why** we are ritualizing this youth's coming of age
☐ What is at the **HEART ♥** of the event/celebration
☐ Youth's **key values, ideals or philosophy of life**
☐ **What kind of event?** Where? When?
☐ **Decisions confirmed** (What, When, Where, How)
☐ If there is disagreement, we have discussed the issues

CONTENT
☐ **Words** that express what is at the ♥
☐ **Music/gestures/symbols/objects**

FORMAT
☐ **Is coherent** with kind of event/celebration
☐ **Social gathering**
☐ **Reminder list**
☐ If necessary, **we have tested our plan**

PAUSE

REALIZING
Expressing meaning

☐ **Prepare setting** (youth/adult/parents)

☐ **Open event** (youth/adult/parents)
☐ **Ritualizing** (Content + Format)
☐ **Leadership coherent** with kind of event/celebration
☐ **Close formal part of event** (youth/adult)

☐ **Social gathering** (all)
☐ **Close event and clean up** (youth/adult/parents/all)

DURATION OF EVENT (suggested)
Ceremony (5–15 minutes)
Social gathering (2–4 hours)

April 2016. This checklist is not intended to be comprehensive. Modifications to fit specific situations are encouraged.

ASHOKA®

7

COMING OF AGE

'Where should I go?' – Alice

'That depends on where you want to end up.' – The Cheshire Cat

Lewis Carroll (1832–98)

Coming of age is one of the most dreamed about, intriguing and exciting transitions in life. Throughout the ages, across all continents and cultures, folktales illustrate the allure of young adulthood. Up to the late modern period, this fascination was counterbalanced by respect for the wisdom of the elders. Present-day obsession with youthfulness makes it difficult to believe that only a few generations ago men powdered their wigs grey and women lied about their age in order to appear older and wiser. While in many parts of the world marriage still marks coming of age, in modern Western societies, the two events are no longer connected.

Many experts consider traditional initiatory rites of passage[1] imperative for moving from youth to adulthood. According to ritual studies expert Ronald Grimes, initiation as a rite of passage 'raises a thicket of problems', not least of which is 'its absence, disappearance or invisibility' in Western disaggregated societies. Many traditional rites hinder intergenerational bonding or are 'so ethereal that they fail to connect with the bodily realities and spiritual needs of those who undergo them' (Grimes 2002, p.100).

---

1   When anthropologist and folklorist Arnold van Gennep (1873–1957) published *Les Rites de Passage* (1909), the book immediately captured the imagination of his contemporaries. He appealingly, but mistakenly, modelled all lifecycle transition ceremonies on the initiation rites of young males as practised in certain small indigenous cultures. His specious model – broken down into three phases that resemble the sequences of a folktale – still confounds the creation of new rituals today.

Hunter-gatherers were dedicated to social bonding, observes anthropologist Matthieu Smyth, yet, as societies stratified, rites of initiation turned into brutal, cruel and humiliating instruments for dominance (2017). While risk-taking is part of life and an important factor in growing up, risky traumatizing initiation rites are neither appropriate nor effective as finishing schools for young people today. Neurologically, the teenage years are an unstable period of development. Judgement and organizational skills are not fully developed, identity is in flux, and there is frequently a significant amount of peer pressure.

The transition into adulthood is not identified by an obvious threshold like birth, marriage, death, or even a birthday. Biological (puberty), social (legal coming of age) and ritual (cultural/religious) adulthood rarely coincide. Informally, young people are initiated into adulthood every single day through their challenges and accomplishments. It is simply a question of taking the time to recognize the challenges and to value the accomplishments. Breaking the transition to adulthood into phases takes into account the youth's situation, interests and evolving maturity.

Formal rites of passage can be a meaningful way of marking some of the transitions. Every spring in Norway more than 10,000 15-year-olds celebrate their coming of age in a 60-year-old secular rite of passage. Throughout the winter they meet in groups to discuss questions such as 'How should we behave towards one another in a changing world?' In addition to learning about critical thinking, ethical issues, human rights and humanism, they socialize during weekend gatherings in nature and at mountain or seaside resorts. The ceremony is a highpoint for the young people, but also for their families. Validation of the process by significant adults is important; by recognizing this fundamental change in the family system, it anchors maturing youth more firmly to their evolving roles as adults.

Figure 7.1. Coming of age
The young person is surrounded by parents, family members and friends. Although friends often exercise greater influence than parents, validation by the latter facilitates the transition to adulthood.

SEVEN SITUATIONS

AMELIA

On the day of her 14th birthday Amelia made a meal (for significant adults) and had a sleepover (with friends) to mark her transition into *puberty*. With her godmother's help she highlighted three core values to cultivate in her adult life: 'doing my best', a sense of humour and friendship. Amelia asked all of her guests to arrive with three jokes. The significant adults in her life (grandparents, godparents and her gymnastics coach) were invited for the evening meal at home. Amelia made up a menu with her favourite foods, shopped, prepared the entire meal and dressed the table. Dessert – a birthday cake made by her father – was served when her girlfriends arrived. After Amelia blew out her candles, her godmother talked about the work they had done together to identify the young girl's values and to prepare the event. As Amelia served the cake, she talked about how much she valued doing a good job, her friends and a sense of humour. She wanted to laugh more often, especially at her own mistakes.

She invited her guests to tell their best joke. The girls then left with Amelia's godmother to go bowling. On their return home, they watched a show with Amelia's favourite stand-up comic.

JONATHAN

Jonathan's father runs a garage, and his mother is the only paediatrician in the rather remote area where they live. From a young age, Jonathan was fascinated by far-away peoples and places. When he was ten years old, he announced he would travel around the world. When, at age 16, he told his parents that he nearly had enough money for his flight, they realized that their son's wanderlust was not just a passing fancy.

Torn between their fears for his safety and supporting him in his dream, his parents asked him to get the best preparation possible. Jonathan enlisted the help of his geography teacher who soon became a family friend. Over the next four years, Jonathan proved himself by organizing short trips, first for his family, then alone. When he turned 20, he set off for two months on his first *solo adventure*. By age 23, Jonathan had realized his dream of circling the globe.

LEO

After searching for three months, Leo got his *first job* at age 18 in a fast-food restaurant. Negotiating his own schedule, getting up early and returning late without any help or reminders from his parents made him feel more grown up. To celebrate his first job, Leo's parents invited him to a nice restaurant. After dessert they asked him how he was holding up. Leo remarked: 'I'm often tired, because I can't spend half the weekend sleeping, but I'm glad for the experience.' His parents praised him for his newly acquired organizational skills and observed that he complained less when things did not go exactly as he would like.

VINCENT

Vincent decided to get the first four months of his obligatory Swiss *military service* out of the way before starting university. The first weeks were the hardest. He had to get used to being woken up at five in the morning or in the middle of the night, getting his equipment together and being ready to move out in a matter of minutes. He did not appreciate the food, the repetitive menial chores, living in barracks with dozens of men, the long hot marches and many other physical challenges.

Vincent said he impressed himself by learning how to ensure the success of a mission efficiently, without panicking. He definitely felt more organized, self-confident and ready for the academic challenges ahead. His father praised his son for the way he pitched in with chores. He no longer had to leave to-do lists for Vincent, because he could see for himself what needed to be done at home.

JESSICA

Jessica became disabled when she was 14 years old. Rehabilitation was long and painful. At first, her friends and family visited and called on her often. As time passed, the number of visits dwindled. Lonely weeks and months blurred into each other. For two years Jessica could not attend school or participate in activities with her teenage friends.

At 17, Jessica felt out of step with her peers and preferred the company of older friends. Although she did not want to have to ever relive such isolation, Jessica recognized that she had benefited from the experience. She said she felt more self-confident and patient with others. According to her family, Jessica was more *mature and independent* than her cousins of the same age. They said her disposition was sunnier than before the accident.

THE HAAS FAMILY

Marine Haas contacted me with a request for an 'end of mothering ritual'. To discuss what she had in mind, I invited her and her husband Joel to come and talk about what they felt was needed. Marine explained that both of their children, Karen and Sam, 24 and 22 years old, still lived at home. Although she had a hard time delegating tasks like cooking and laundry that she had assumed for years, she also resented having to do them alone now that there were four adults in the house.

A date five weeks hence was chosen for the ritualization, and all four of them went to work on their contributions. The family invited 15 close friends, including the children's godparents and their families.

Marine started the evening off by asking everyone to sit on the floor in front of the washing machine. As she handed around small cups of warm aniseed milk, a drink she had often served the children in the evening, Marine expressed her pleasure at being the mother of two such lovely children. Then, to peals of laughter, she estimated how many loads of washing and how many shirts, trousers and socks she had washed and folded over the years. As a follow-up to these calculations, she tendered her resignation as chief cook and laundry woman.

The sun was setting as everyone trooped upstairs. Joel read a poem he had written for his wife, renewing his commitment to her. Karen and Sam each brought out a shoe box filled with little papier-mâché figurines they had made, and told funny stories remembered from their childhood. They expressed their *gratitude* to their parents for all they had done for them, and offered them the boxes. One of the guests played the piano to accompany the group as they sang songs from their group's camping trips. The evening ended with a splendid meal prepared and served by Joel. All four pitched in for the clean-up.

A few weeks into the planning of the ceremony, Sam suddenly announced to his parents that he had decided to study abroad. He left home a few weeks after the event. Two months later, Karen moved in with her boyfriend.

BETH

Randall, Beth's father, wanted to do something special for his daughter's 18th birthday. Yet nothing he proposed seemed to suit her. Beth explained that she and her friends preferred living in the moment and improvising to well-planned, supposedly meaningful events.

Nonetheless, with Beth's permission, Randall organized a small party for his daughter with close family members, including Beth's favourite cousins, one of whom had her birthday the same week. During a *ceremonial moment*, Beth and her cousin both received mock diplomas followed by high acclaim and silly prizes for real and imagined qualities such as creativity, tenacity and patience, as well as a good appetite, the ability to sleep anywhere and longevity. In turn, the two girls spontaneously expressed their gratitude to each person present for qualities they particularly appreciated or support they had received from those present.

On the day of Beth's 18th birthday, her father offered her a gift: a lovely pen engraved with her name. As a new adult, Randall explained, the pen would remind her of her new rights and responsibilities, among which was the right to sign contracts. Beth was delighted by the pen, and appreciated the reminder.

CHECKLIST FOR RITUALIZING COMING OF AGE

The checklist serves as a guide for you, the young person coming of age. Choosing an adult you trust to work with you is a wise move. This person can help you keep your objectives in sight as you plan and craft the ritualization. The situations described above may inspire you as you prepare to ritualize this transition.

The planning phase for coming of age celebrations includes only two questions: Who and When? Exploration of Why, What and How are part of the Creating phase. The answers to these three questions determine Where and a more precise time for the event.

PLANNING PHASE

This phase is about brainstorming. These tools are recommended for planning to ritualize with youth:

Questionnaire on ritual identity. See the tool in Chapter 5.

Five techniques for feeling safe. See the tool in Chapter 5.

Prioritizing. See the tool in Chapter 5.

When? (general question)

There is no obvious or ideal time or age for celebrating the transition to adulthood. The passage may be marked as early as age 11 (a girl's first menses) and as late as 26 (first job); sociocultural norms and local customs may generate gender-specific celebrations. Try to tie your event to what is happening in your life. If you play the piano and have an audition soon, this event can serve as a jumping-off point for a coming of age celebration. Those close to you can support you in your success – or temporary setback. If you prefer an initiation-like challenge and have always wanted to go hang-gliding, create an event around it. Graduation from secondary school, trade school or university may also be an ideal occasion for this kind of a celebration.

Who?

You are centre stage during this transition; your family is in the wings.

With whom?

Decide whether to celebrate alone, with friends, with family or a combination of these options. You should be fully consenting and involved in every aspect of the organization. Including your family is advisable, because they can affirm your feeling that something has changed or been achieved. Whatever route you choose, take time to clarify your ties to the people close to you. This may give direction to your choice of event or activity.

PAUSE

CREATING PHASE

Coming of age is a process that is punctuated by a series of events, during which your relationships are renegotiated, until you are seen and accepted as an adult in your own right. At the heart of this passage is the changing relationship between you, your family and society as a whole. You may know instinctively what you want to do to mark these changes; if not, you are not alone. Ritualizing coming of age is uncharted territory in Western societies. Start off by identifying your core values. As with Beth (see 'Seven situations' above), marking this transition may involve more of a 'ceremonial moment' than the organization of a big event.

 Core values. See the tool in Chapter 5.

Why?

This section is designed to help you clarify your intention and goals.

 Mapping it out is a specifically designed decision tool for the creation of coming of age rituals.

 Integrity and *coherence* are essential to the process. Integrity is about honesty and moral principles. Coherence implies a direct link between the event and your personal values. Does your project pass the *Coherence test*?

PAUSE

REALIZING PHASE

The realization of your project depends entirely on the kind of activity you chose to organize.

RISK FACTORS IN CELEBRATING COMING OF AGE

In addition to the risks noted above, self- and peer-initiations are not encouraged, as they can quickly get out of hand. Using rituals from cultures other than one's own dilutes meaningfulness. Moreover, indigenous groups consider the use of their practices by outsiders disrespectful (see the Declaration of war against exploiters of Lakota spirituality in Chapter 3).

CHECKLIST FOR A WEDDING CEREMONY

PLANNING
First things first

☐ We are clear about our objectives for this ceremony

We have identified:

☐ **About whom?** Couple
☐ **By whom?** The couple are responsible for crafting/presiding/organizing
☐ **With whom?** (who participates/is invited)
☐ **What?** Wedding ceremony
☐ **When?** A fitting date/time/duration for the event
☐ **Where?** A suitable place/setting/venue

COMMUNICATION AND CONTINGENCY

☐ We have contacted or invited all (see 'With whom?') noted above
☐ Participants have approved their roles
☐ If there is disagreement about how to proceed we know who makes the final decision
☐ We have contingency plans for with Whom, When and Where

PAUSE

CREATING
Making sense (couple)

We, the craftspeople, are agreed on:

☐ **Why and how** we are ritualizing our union
☐ What is at the **HEART ♥** of this ceremony
☐ The **key values, ideals or philosophy of life** we wish to transmit or convey
☐ **Decisions confirmed** (Who, What, When, Where)
☐ If there is disagreement, we have discussed the issues

CONTENT
☐ **Words ♥** Our vow + texts
☐ **Music**
☐ **Gestures/symbols/objects**

FORMAT
☐ **Entry** into ceremonial space
☐ **Welcome**
☐ **Heart ♥** Our vow + texts
☐ **Closing/exit** ceremonial space > transition
☐ **Social gathering**
☐ **Choreography/scenography** check for visual participation from all seats
☐ **Reminder list**
☐ **We have walked through** the ceremony and checked for flow and choreography

PAUSE

REALIZING
Expressing meaning

☐ **Prepare setting** (couple/presider/organizer)

☐ **Open ceremony** (presider)
☐ **Ritualizing** (Content + Format)
  ♦ Conduct (presider) ♦ Participate (all)
☐ **Close ceremony** (presider)

☐ **Open social part of event** (organizer)
☐ **Social gathering** (all)
☐ **Close event and clean up** (organizer)

DURATION OF EVENT (suggested)

Ceremony (20–40 minutes)
Social gathering (2–6 hours)

April 2016. This checklist is not intended to be comprehensive. Modifications to fit specific situations are encouraged.

ASH◉KA

8

MARRIAGE

I promise to nourish our love with affection, kindness and passion.

To enrich our relationship with a sense of fun, humour and adventure.

I can't wait to share the future with you at my
side through good times and bad.

Andrew and Maureen's wedding vow

Weddings, like many of the major transitions in life, are bittersweet occasions. Something is gained, and something is lost. Love shines on centre stage and loss dries a teary eye in the wings. Marriage may be an affair of the heart, but it is the only lifecycle transition that is also a legal affair: laws decide who marries and who does not.

In the past, when couples married very young (before the age of 21), the wedding served as a coming of age rite for both young people. Their parents took care of marking this transition for their children: the couple's families organized and paid for the wedding. The union was solemnized according to traditional civil and/or religious rites that reflected their parents' values and social positions. The festivities consolidated the new alliances and eased the young couple's transition to independence and married life.

Most couples today see marriage as a choice – their choice – not an obligation. Many live together for years without being married. Some couples do not want the state meddling in their intimate relationships. Others consider legal approval superfluous. Still others face legal, social or financial obstacles to an official union. In some countries, like Switzerland, couples who are married pay higher taxes than those who live together. Many places still do not recognize marriage for same-sex couples. There are often few ties between the couple's families. Many do not share the same cultural or religious heritage. Officially, the average age for getting married has increased by five years[1] since 1970. When they do marry, modern couples assume the organization and the cost of their wedding, with little or no outside help.

Yet, as in the past, the ceremony – without which there is no wedding! – still unites the pair in the eyes of their friends, family and society, and it gives the guests insights into the couple's upbringing, values and social status. The new alliance still involves at least three family groups: the couple's new family unit and their two families of origin. Public recognition of the couple's union still serves to help their families and circle of friends adjust to the implications of their wedded status. As the newly-weds redefine their loyalties to their families of origin, they gain privileged ties to their partner's family group. The reception celebrates these changes.

There are currently three main options for wedding ceremonies: civil, religious or secular. Variants on these options are regulated by the laws of the country or region in which the wedding takes place. In some countries or regions, notably Australia, the United States, Canada and Scotland, an officiant may be licensed to represent the state. In this case, the civil wedding can also be a religious or secular ceremony. In most European countries, a civil wedding ceremony must precede a religious or secular ceremony. For some couples the civil formalities suffice; others feel the need for something more to solemnize their union.

Secular celebrants that represent humanist groups and indie (independent) celebrants may offer adaptable albeit ready-made or tailor-made ceremonies. The celebrants help the couple clarify their shared identity, values and common goals as they take this step together. There

---

[1]   On average, in New Zealand, women marry at the age of 26 and men at 27; in the United States and Canada, women marry at the age of 27 and men at 29; in Australia, Switzerland and South Africa, women marry at the age of 30 and men at 33; in the UK, France and Ireland, women marry at the age of 32 and men at 33.

is nothing like an authentic wedding to rally the support of families and friends and to anchor the couple in a new reality.

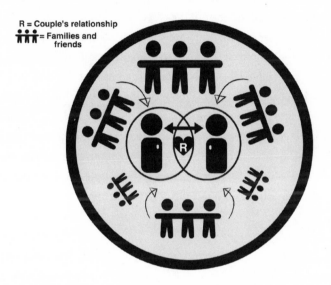

Figure 8.1. Marriage
The couple's relationship is at the heart of their wedding ceremony. They are surrounded and supported by their parents, family members and friends.

FIVE SITUATIONS

ALEX AND KRYSTEN

Krysten is a Unitarian Universalist. Alex had done a doctorate on Tibetan Buddhism. This young Californian couple chose to celebrate their union in a small village in Burgundy, France, where Alex's uncle and his friend ran a bed-and-breakfast. Around 30 of their relatives and closest friends travelled there for the wedding. The ceremony was held in the woods in the village *lavoir* (covered wash house). Early in the day, the couple's friends and family decorated the *lavoir* with flowers, tea candles in yogurt pots and vines from the forest. An acoustic guitarist and the gurgling of the fountain accompanied Alex as he lead their guests into the *lavoir*, lit the first tea candle and placed it gently onto the surface of the water.

The guests followed his example or scattered flower petals before taking their places in a circle around the large stone wash basin.

Everyone stood for Krysten's entry into the ceremonial space. Tibetan bells were rung to signal the start of the ceremony. A ball of yellow string was passed among the guests, and I spoke of how this Buddhist symbol from Alex's work symbolized their ties to each other and of Krysten and Alex's bond in marriage. Each person cut off a bit of string and tied it onto their neighbour's wrist as a symbol of their support for the newly-weds. The bride and groom tied bits of string onto each other's wrists as a symbol of their commitment to each other. After they had exchanged their vows and wedding rings, Tibetan bells were rung again to signal the end of the ceremony. After a few group pictures, the couple and their guests walked back to the village for a reception and dancing in the village hall.

MICHEL AND ADRIENNE

Michel and Adrienne are a Swiss couple who live and work in New York. Their friends and families celebrated their union with them in a remote spot in the Alps high above Zermatt (Switzerland). The couple chose these key words: Love, Trust, Source, Respect and Togetherness.

WEDDING VOW

I promise to accept you as you are, to help you in difficult times and support you in whatever you undertake.

I promise to cultivate the world of togetherness, respect and trust that we have built together, and to be your partner in our joint projects.

I promise to nurture our love, to be your haven of peace and tenderness, as well as your source of strength, energy and inspiration.

A year later, the three of us met up at their home in New York. The couple talked about how glad they were that they had taken the time to better understand their relationship, and how it served them now with their first child.

ALICE AND SANDRA

Alice and Sandra invited their guests to the comfort and intimacy of their home in Rhode Island to witness the joining of their lives in marriage. The wedding ceremony represented public recognition of the couple's private experience of committed partnership over more than three decades.

WEDDING VOW

I ask you to be no other than yourself, loving what I do know of you, trusting what I don't yet know, respecting your integrity, and in holding faith in your love for me. For as long as we live, and in all that life may bring us, I accept you as my partner in this life.

EXCHANGE OF RINGS

Alice/Sandra, with this ring I marry you, and to you I will be true so long as we both shall live.

NEVILLE AND MINA

Neville's mother is British, and his father is from India. Mina's father is Swiss, and her mother is from Japan. The couple wanted their wedding ceremony to be about their relationship and their hopes for the future. It was also important for them to honour their respective families' traditions, in particular the traditions of family members who travelled far to join them on their wedding day. Two symbolic gestures were integrated into their ceremony. The first was a Zoroastrian ritual known as 'Lighting the spiritual flame', traditionally performed at the beginning of Parsee wedding ceremonies. Neville's cousin carried the lamp or *devo* into the ceremonial space. Neville and Mina asked me to explain to their guests that they lit the lamp together to honour Neville's father's family and their traditions. It was a symbol of their desire to work together and jointly light and tend the spiritual fire of their union. In honour of Mina's mother and her family, the wedding ended with a Shinto ceremony, known as 'San san kudo', during which the couple drank small cups of sake. Two of Mina's cousins, dressed in traditional kimonos, presided at the Shinto ceremony.

A PERFECT FIT BY NEVILLE

Life begins with discovery,
Stubborn, selfish, reckless one can be.

Seasons pass and still no mend
Until comes a different friend

A special friend bringing sense to life
A partner, an angel, a loving wife

An understanding of completeness
A realization that one was not
A new discovery, a new life
Foundations you have got.

How lucky you are to have found each other
Everything seems to fit
Cheek to cheek, hand in hand
Both ready to commit.

Trust and respect so evident
A powerful union flourishing
The fusion which you make today
Ensures nothing is missing.

WEDDING VOW

I promise to trust you, be faithful to you and never doubt our love.

I promise to respect you, support you and take care of you at all times.

I promise to nourish the love we have for each other so that it may grow and mature alongside us.

AMANDA AND JULIAN

Amanda's parents are of Spanish and Swiss origin. She had just earned her doctorate in philosophy. Julian studied biology, and his parents are Dutch. Their friends joke about Amanda's large collection of books and comics, and Julian is known for his love of fantasy worlds. The couple chose to translate a text from one of Amanda's favourite comic books and have it read by a friend. They told their guests that they hoped to be able to apply these seven rules to their life as a married couple and to teach them to their children.

Always remember these seven basic rules in your search for wisdom[2]:

1. Look for the good in everything. Forgive even the most terrible mistakes, but never forget.

2. Strike only when necessary. Burn, but not excessively, never be cruel.

3. When you find true friendship, cherish it and consider it sacred. There is nothing better than a lasting friendship.

4. Face reality, but also let yourself enjoy fantasy and fables. It will help you grow, both within yourself and around you.

5. Replace any sod you might have displaced during your journey. Move along quietly and without fuss, but do let the world know you're travelling through.

6. Respect your code, your ideals, your reputation, and make them your steadfast values.

7. Above all, follow your heart. Laugh and sing. Be generous to yourself and always ask the best of your body and your mind.

After saying their vows, the couple exchanged rings to tinkling music from the video game 'The Legend of Zelda', Koji Kondo's 'Great Fairy Fountain Theme'.

---

2 Nathan Never's seven rules were translated from Serra (1996).

'Our guests were touched by our wedding ceremony', the couple wrote a year later. 'It really was at the heart of our wedding, and definitely contributed to its success. We have a baby girl on the way, due in June, and are very excited!'

CHECKLIST FOR A WEDDING CEREMONY

Your ceremony is one of a kind. It has never been done before and will never be done again.

Allot six to twelve months for the crafting of your wedding ceremony. Answering the questions in the planning phase – What, Who, When and Where – may take a few minutes, or much longer. The same goes for the creating phase when you explore the questions Why and How. The realizing phase involves setting up, the ceremony, the social gathering and the clean-up. A well-constructed wedding ceremony lasts from 20–40 minutes.

PLANNING PHASE

Planning begins early for many couples, especially for those who want a popular venue. Give yourselves the time you need to clarify your shared identity, values and common goals. The weeks running up to the wedding are filled with unexpected details that only you can sort out. Try to put the finishing touches on your ceremony six to eight weeks before your date. These tools are for crafting your ceremony:

Questionnaire on ritual identity. See the tool in Chapter 5.

Prioritizing helps you decide who participates in your ceremony, who will be invited to your wedding.

Who presides? In most cases, one of the parents, a relative or a friend can preside.

Who?

Your relationship is at the centre of your marriage (see Figure 8.1). Together you are responsible for planning and crafting your wedding ceremony.

When?

Is there perhaps a date and/or time that is significant for the two of you or that marks an important chapter in your relationship? Check with a few key people like parents, grandparents, siblings and those you want in your wedding party to make sure they are free to participate.

Where?

Choose a venue for your wedding ceremony in which you both feel comfortable. Is the setting adapted to the kind of activities you planned? Can your programme proceed in the venue in fair and foul weather? Consider ecological issues related to the venue such as travel distance, decorations and catering. Is the venue accessible and safe for all of the guests you invited (elderly, disabled and small children)?

PAUSE

CREATING PHASE

The most touching and sincere ceremonies are composed entirely of original material. You do not need stock vows or to scour the internet for overused texts by others that express their views of love and marriage. Your friends and families' views on these subjects are great for the wedding reception but inappropriate at your ceremony. Creating material for your wedding that makes sense simply involves calling on the artist in you. Let these tools guide you as you explore together what makes sense to you.

 Core values is about what forms the pillars of your relationship.

 The *Coherence test* assesses the choices you made in the planning phase in light of your core values.

 Why and how? is a base for your discussions about how you imagine your wedding.

Content

The content of your ceremony is centred round your key words or values, and ripples out from there. One couple who chose 'respect' and 'listening' illustrated this with a short paragraph about their habit of spending 15 minutes together after work to talk about their day. One groom, a mathematician, wrote a text about circles which began 'A circle is a series of points...', then talked about the importance of their circles of families and friends. Let your values inspire you as you determine which words, music and gestures to use, then check to be sure they are coherent with your values.

 Plumbing the meaning of core values is about writing wedding vows and original material that highlight your relationship (see Figure 8.2). Strive for simplicity: your promise may be as simple as this: 'My love [or Name], I promise to nourish our love/marriage through...[list of your key words].'

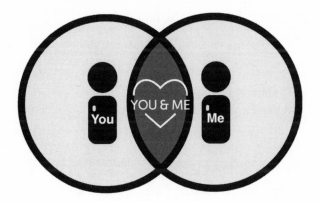

Figure 8.2. You and me
The couple's relationship is at the heart of the wedding ceremony. Their shared values and aspirations are showcased in their vows and texts.

The situations described above may inspire you as you write your joint wedding vows and texts together, using the words and themes you identified as representing your shared values.

 Just the right music. See the tool in Chapter 5.

 Small gestures, big impact. See the tool in Chapter 5.

Format

The format or order of your ceremony represents the framework for your content. Once you have all the elements together, put them in the order that makes the most sense to you.

Format of the ceremony. See the tool in Chapter 5.

Sample order of a wedding ceremony

- *Entrance music* – guests gather for the ceremony; participants and parents enter the ceremonial space; the couple enter, separately or together
- *Welcome and explanations* – celebrant
- *Readings* – friends and relatives (alternate with 30–60 seconds of music)
- *Partners confirm their intention to marry*
- *Taking turns the couple recite a special text for their partner*
- *Joint wedding vow*
- *Symbolic gesture of the vow* (wedding rings, kiss)
- *Closing words* – celebrant
- *Exit music* – the couple leave the ceremonial space followed by their guests

PAUSE

REALIZING PHASE

Public wedding ceremonies are intense and emotional, not simply because they transmit meaning from the couple to each one of the guests, but because they let everyone present know about the couple.

 Ritualizing, step by step. See the tool in Chapter 5.

 Guidelines for readers serves to prepare your friends and family members for reading aloud in the context of a wedding ceremony.

RISK FACTORS IN CRAFTING
A WEDDING CEREMONY

The two greatest obstacles to a meaningful wedding ceremony are mistaken ritual identity and underestimating the time it takes to create a bespoke ceremony.

Costumed theme weddings, wedding ceremonies that borrow rituals and symbols from foreign traditions, religious ceremonies for the non-religious and vice versa are all to be avoided, because they give an inadequate picture of the couple's relationship and how they envisage their future together. Couples who do not share religious, philosophical or cultural backgrounds do best with an indie celebrant with experience in crafting weddings that take these challenges into account.[3]

---

3   For more on crafting ceremony as a multicultural couple, see 'Multicultural Wedding Ceremonies. A Journey into the World of Diversity' by Andrés Allemand Smaller (2017).

CHECKLIST FOR RITUALIZING GROWING UP AND GROWING OLD

PLANNING
First things first

□ We are clear about our objectives for this event

We have identified:

□ **About whom?** The person at the centre of ritualization
□ **By whom?** Who is **responsible for crafting/ organizing/presiding?**
□ **With whom?** Who **participates/is invited**
□ **What?** Define the occasion
□ **When?** Determine **date/time/duration**
□ **Where?** Choose **place/setting/venue**

COMMUNICATION AND CONTINGENCY

□ We have contacted or invited all ('With whom?') noted above
□ Participants have approved their roles
□ If there is disagreement about how to proceed we know who makes the final decision
□ We have contingency plans and leeway for timing

 PAUSE

CREATING
Making sense (person at centre of ritual)

We, the craftspeople, are agreed on:

□ **Why and how** we ritualize this passage or event
□ What is at the **HEART ♥** of the event/celebration
□ The **key values, ideals or philosophy of life** we wish to convey
□ **Decisions confirmed** (Who, What, When, Where)
□ If there is disagreement, we have discussed the issues

CONTENT

□ **Words** that express what is at the ♥
□ **Music/gestures/symbols/objects**

FORMAT

□ Is **coherent** with kind of event/celebration
□ **Social gathering**
□ **Reminder list**
□ If necessary, **we have tested our plan**

 PAUSE

REALIZING
Expressing meaning

□ **Prepare setting** (person ritualizing transition)

□ **Open event** (person ritualizing/presider)
□ **Ritualizing** (Content + Format)
□ **Leadership coherent** with kind of event/ celebration
□ **Close formal part** (person ritualizing/presider)

□ **Social gathering** (all)
□ **Close event and clean up** (person ritualizing/all)

DURATION OF EVENT (suggested)
Ceremony (to be determined)
Social gathering (2–4 hours)

April 2016. This checklist is not intended to be comprehensive. Modifications to fit specific situations are encouraged.

9

GROWING UP, GROWING OLD

Confucius (551–479 BCE) said:

'At fifteen my heart-and-mind were set on learning;
at thirty I took my stance;
at forty I was no longer of two minds;
at fifty I realized the *ming* of *t'ien*,[1]
at sixty my ear was attuned;
At seventy I could give my heart-and-mind free reign
Without overstepping the mark.'

Analects, 2/4

HAPPY BIRTHDAY!

Birthdays seem ever so far apart to children, and ever so close together to the elderly. Whether we are excited about our upcoming birthday or dread it depends not only on our age but also on how we view life. The adage 'growing old is mandatory, growing up is optional' makes us smile and wonder if growing up and happiness are at all compatible. To the question, 'why grow up?' philosopher Susan Neiman replies:

The short answer is: because it is harder than you think, so hard that it can amount to resistance. The forces that shape our world

---

[1] In this context, I understand *'ming* of *t'ien'* to refer to Confucius' sense of having achieved emotional attunement both between himself and others (i.e. harmony in communication) and between his own values and higher laws (heavens, the Tao).

are no more interested in real grown-ups than they were in Kant's
day, for children make more compliant subjects (and consumers).
(2014, p.162)

According to researchers, the nadir of unhappiness varies from country to
country: Ukrainians are at their most miserable at the age of 62 and the
Swiss at 35. The global average age for unhappiness is 46. People in
the majority of the 72 countries studied hit their unhappiest time in their
forties and early fifties (*The Economist* 2010). If unhappiness is something
we eventually 'grow' out of, can we grow into happiness?

Sustainable happiness, says writer Sarah van Gelder, is a 'form of
happiness that endures, through good times and bad because it starts
with the fundamental requirements and aspirations of being human'. It is
'built on a healthy natural world and a vibrant and fair society' (2014, p.1).
Being fully human means living creatively to meet our basic needs for food,
drink, clothing and shelter, but also making even ordinary days special
through play, art and ritual. It means teaching our children that gifts do
not make a birthday happy, about leave-taking and civilized behaviour.
The basic requirement for civilization is not economic growth but safety.
People must feel safe to optimize their potential and be creative,[2] observes
scientist Stephen Porges (2012). When we feel safe we can creatively
contribute to the world and make sense of our lives: we can be happy.
'The good life isn't a place at which you arrive', says Jonathan Fields, 'it's
the lens through which you see and create your world' (2011–15).

Growing up and growing old is about savouring everyday moments by
making them special. These moments include birthdays, anniversaries as
well as the darker days set apart by sickness and loss. The situations
described below show how a few people turned those smaller transitions
into something special.

---

2   Porges' research shows that the neurophysiological processes associated with
feeling safe are a prerequisite for social behaviour. They access both the higher brain
structures that enable humans to be creative and generative and also the lower
brain structures involved in regulating health, growth and restoration.

Figure 9.1. Growing up, growing old
Growing up and growing old is a series of moments like pearls on a necklace, each one more precious than the last.

NINE SITUATIONS

MATTHEW

The first day of school in the Williams family follows a well-known pattern, so Matthew, the youngest of four, knows what awaits him. The night before his first day at school, Matthew takes a bath and then lays out his new clothes and shoes. Seeing his serious face at breakfast, Matthew's brothers tease him and try to make him laugh. Both of his parents accompany Matthew to school. As they are waiting on the playground, his grandparents arrive and give Matthew a new backpack. As Matthew joins the other students, he turns around one last time to wave goodbye to his parents and grandparents. Before heading off to work, the boys' parents and grandparents have coffee together and reminisce about other first days of school.

NINA

Six-and-a-half-year-old Nina pestered her parents for a two-wheel bicycle. They wanted to wait until her birthday. Then Nina fell quite ill with the chicken pox, and her little brother caught it too. It was a trying time for the family. When both children had recovered, Nina's parents noticed that Nina seemed more grown up. Even though it was not yet her birthday, her parents decided to mark this change in Nina with a pink bicycle.

STEVEN

Nine-year-old Steven did not have an easy time at school. His confidence was at a low point when his family decided to make a 125km trek in the Himalayas. Their warm clothes and sleeping bags were carried by porters, but everyone in the group, including Steven, carried their own day pack with a windbreaker, a sweater, a change of socks, a bottle of water, a small snack and a whistle, in case someone got separated from the group. Steven did well, walking six to eight hours a day for ten days on a trail that rose and dipped constantly. On the last leg of the journey, the group congratulated Steven for his considerable efforts and for being a good sport and such a pleasant travel companion. One trekker noted that Steven's confidence in himself seemed to grow as his slim legs got stronger. Steven chose to celebrate his accomplishment with a yak steak.

THEA

When Susan, a single mother, noticed that her daughter Thea would soon have her first period, she knew that she should prepare her daughter for the event, but felt inadequate and ambivalent. A friend recommended a mother–daughter workshop called 'Jumping over the Moon' offered by a nurse who specializes in women's issues and natural contraception. Susan and Thea joined a dozen other mother–daughter dyads to learn about the physiological, psychological and even symbolic influences of a woman's menstrual cycle on her life. At the end of the day, Susan and Thea had a new language for what was about to happen, and new friends to accompany them as they moved into this new phase in Thea's life.

THE TAYLOR FAMILY

Every Tuesday night the newly composed family – Eric and his two daughters, aged 12 and 15 and Mary and her two boys, aged 13 and 16 – meet for a meal together. At first, each parent prepared the meal with his or her children and the other 'team' took care of the clean-up. At the end of each Tuesday night meal, after determining the menu for the following week, they reserved 15 minutes for talking about the family calendar and holiday projects and addressed any difficulties that arose, either between the children or between the two families. After about six months, the children told their parents that they wanted to mix the teams. The Tuesday meal became a time to catch up with each other, to relax, and also served as a safety valve for the children and their parents.

MAX AND SUE

After five years of marriage, Max and Sue admitted that their intimate relationship had come to an end. Max jokingly proposed they have a 'last supper' as husband and wife. The idea of a special dinner struck home, because neither wanted to abandon their friendship. As Max cooked, Sue prepared two small boxes she called their treasure chests. During the meal they celebrated the connection they had enjoyed. To ritualize this process, and provide some containment, they took it in turns to speak and place in the other's chest a note, small object or picture that illustrated an experience or time they held dear. There was surprise and laughter as they acknowledged their powerful connection. Over coffee, to prevent them from falling back into their old roles, they established rules for the new boundaries of their relationship. They also talked about how they could move towards this new way of being together. Putting the lid on the boxes at the end and having a tangible reminder of their last supper felt important.

BONNIE

Several months before Bonnie's 60th birthday, she decided to realize a childhood dream that she said 'had haunted me my whole life: I wanted to learn to tap dance. I had wanted to tap dance ever since I was five years old!... Once I decided to act on my dream, the rest was easy. Within days I found a class with a teacher who was delighted to also give me private lessons, and two months later I danced the "Razzle Dazzle" from the film "Chicago" for my birthday guests.'

MARTIN

Martin came to see me six months before his retirement from professional life as a teacher. He felt lucky to have had a profession that he enjoyed, but he was concerned about how he would react in the autumn after 61 years of life dictated by the school calendar. The idea of doing nothing was inconceivable.

We talked about his inclination to fill his life with projects or volunteer work. I encouraged him to see the winter as a period of gestation during which his desire for future activities could ripen. He identified two projects: a vacation with his wife in October and the organization of a large family party in December. Then he compiled a list of activities that he enjoyed: walks with his dog, theatre, sleeping in an extra hour in the mornings. Finally, he sketched out a sample weekly then monthly schedule. When we met again in January to take stock of the situation, Martin told me that he was glad he had prepared for this transition. He was thoroughly enjoying his new use of time. So much so, in fact, that he was not sure whether or not he would join two newly retired friends in a tutoring project.

VERA AND WALT

Vera is 77 years old, and Walt just turned 93. They celebrated Walt's birthday with a weekend trip to a historical site Vera loves. 'We have been lovers for 25 years', they say. 'We feel so lucky to have each other. Every day we spend hours talking, holding each other, laughing – we savour every single moment.'

CHECKLIST FOR RITUALIZING GROWING UP AND GROWING OLD

Celebrations for these 'minor' transitions in life are usually more informal than a wedding or a funeral. The preparing and realizing phases are clearly laid out in Chapter 5. The two tools below are probably the most practical for the creating phase, but you should feel free to use any of the tools you need from the Toolbox to craft your event.

 Core values. See the tool in Chapter 5.

 Coherence test. See the tool in Chapter 5.

CHECKLIST FOR A FUNERAL CEREMONY

PLANNING
First things first

- [ ] We are clear about our objectives for this ceremony

We have identified:

- [ ] **About whom?** The deceased, his/her life and relationships
- [ ] **By whom? Close family and friends** are responsible for **crafting/presiding/organizing**
- [ ] **With whom?** Who **participates/is invited**
- [ ] **What?** Funeral
- [ ] **When?** Determine date/time/duration
- [ ] **Where?** A suitable place/setting/venue

COMMUNICATION AND CONTINGENCY

- [ ] We have contacted or invited all ('With whom?') noted above
- [ ] Participants have approved their roles
- [ ] If there is **disagreement** about how to proceed we know who makes the final decision
- [ ] We have contingency plans for When, Where, What

PAUSE

CREATING
Making sense (craftspeople)

We, the craftspeople, are agreed on:

- [ ] **Why and how** we ritualize our loved one's passing
- [ ] Deceased is at the **HEART ♥** of this ceremony
- [ ] The deceased's **key values, ideals or philosophy of life** (in the case of a baby, the parents' values)
- [ ] **Decisions confirmed** (Who, What, When, Where)
- [ ] If there is disagreement, we have discussed the issues

CONTENT

- [ ] **Words ♥ Homage + tributes**
- [ ] **Music**
- [ ] **Symbols/objects**
- [ ] **Gesture of separation**

FORMAT

- [ ] **Entry** into ceremonial space
- [ ] **Welcome**
- [ ] **Heart ♥ Homage + tributes**
- [ ] **Closing/exit** ceremonial space > transition
- [ ] **Social gathering**
- [ ] Choreography/scenography
- [ ] Reminder list
- [ ] We have checked for flow and choreography

PAUSE

REALIZING
Expressing meaning

- [ ] **Prepare setting** (presider/participants)
- [ ] **Open ceremony** (presider)
- [ ] **Ritualizing** (Content + Format)
  ♦ Conduct (presider) ♦ Participate (all)
- [ ] **Close ceremony** (presider)
- [ ] **Open social part of event** (presider)
- [ ] **Social gathering** (all)
- [ ] **Close event and clean up** (organizer)

DURATION OF EVENT (suggested)
Ceremony (20–50 minutes)
Social gathering (1–3 hours)

April 2016. This checklist is not intended to be comprehensive. Modifications to fit specific situations are encouraged.

10

DEATH AND ENDINGS

Oh how wrong you are
to think that the years
will never end.
We must die.

Life is a dream,
that seems so sweet,
but joy is all too brief.
We must die.
Of no avail is medicine,
of no use is quinine,
we cannot be cured.
We must die...

We die singing,
we die playing
the cittern, the bagpipes, yet
die we must.
We die dancing,
drinking, eating;
with this carrion,
die we must...

Anonymous lyrics of 17th-century music known as Passacaglia della vita

Each one of us has a deeply human story of love and hope, of encounters and disappearances, of life and death. Life has a beginning, a middle and an end. Death represents that inconceivable final chapter. Funerals help us come to terms, not with death per se, but with the fact that death is part of life. They initiate a process that allows the bereaved to loosen their ties with the deceased, adapt to a new reality without their loved one and reweave the fabric of their daily lives as best they can around an irremediable absence.

The disparity between expectations and funeral practices in Western societies has widened remarkably over the last 20 years. While the majority of people choose a personalized celebration of their life, most funerals are still traditional or religious; a growing number forego ceremony all together, particularly in major European urban areas.[1] In a recent study of the bereaved in Great Britain, 'just 1% admitted to knowing all the deceased's funeral preferences, with 31% having no idea whether their loved one would have wished to be buried or cremated, and 53% uncertain about whether to hold a religious or non-religious service' (SunLife 2015).

In response to the increase in demand for non-religious funerals, some celebrants and funeral directors now propose a repertoire of 'traditional ceremonies'. Sociologist Margaret Holloway observes that expectations for authenticity and meaning are higher for these reinvented or customized traditions; the ceremonies need to be right. She quotes a mourner as saying 'funerals aren't nice but it couldn't have been nicer' (2015). What happens if a funeral is not right or nice? There is one church funeral I will never forget. As we stood around the open grave, a cousin of the deceased announced: 'Her husband was cremated; I'm sure she wanted cremation too.' A nursing home representative finally spoke up: 'Her intake file states no preference for either burial or cremation.' The funeral director nodded, and the gravediggers lowered her casket into the ground.

---

1   In 2010, about 40–50 per cent of those who died in the larger cities of Europe did not have religious services. In Paris, well over 30 per cent of the dead went directly from the morgue to the cemetery or to the crematorium with no ceremony whatsoever (Gairin 2010, p.96). The percentage of Americans for whom a religious component in their funeral is 'not at all important' has more than doubled in the last three years, from 10 to 21 per cent (National Funeral Directors Association's Report 2015). A study in Great Britain (IMC Research 2010) revealed that, while 54 per cent of respondents preferred a personalized celebration of their life and only 27 per cent a traditional funeral, the majority of all funerals are religious or traditional. Only 20 per cent of the 18–24s wanted traditional ceremonies; this rose to 40 per cent for the over-65s.

A funeral is right when it fits so well that the bereaved recognize the deceased in the ceremony and have no regrets about the decisions made. Inappropriate funerary rituals can hamper mourning. Marie-Frédérique Bacqué, clinical psychologist and thanatologist in Canada, says:

> In Quebec, psychologists work with the families to develop personalized ceremonies to deal with their grief. These are very compelling initiatives... The fear of death is inherent in our human condition, and nothing can ever erase it. But we can make this fear more bearable by containing it in rites and breaking the silence that surrounds it... Talking about the inevitability of death enables us to create benchmarks that mitigate the trauma. This in turn helps to reassure us about what will happen to us once we have left the category of the living. (2010)

Funerals are performed for the dead, but are essentially for the living. Being right and nice is not about having a perfect ceremony, or about novelty. It is about sensemaking. Ready-made religious or traditional funerals are suitable for members of an institution, secular or religious. The rest of us require tailor-made funerals. There is a dearth of people trained to accompany the bereaved as they craft a secular bespoke funeral. This chapter proposes concrete tools that encourage relatives and friends to become more intuitive and confident in their decision-making around the funeral of a loved one.

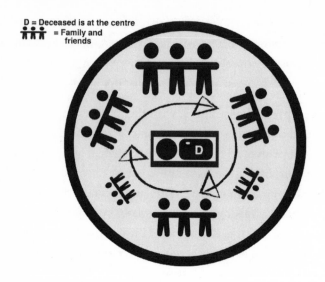

Figure 10.1. Funerals
Death represents the end of life but also the end of a relationship. The funeral is a time for honouring the deceased and his or her life as well as what they meant to us.

SEVEN SITUATIONS

ETHAN

Ethan died in hospital when he was four years old while awaiting a liver transplant. His family had spent most of his short life at his bedside. They knew his life hung by a thread, but kept hoping for a miracle. They were devastated by Ethan's death. As they planned his funeral, they told stories about their short time together, and finally decided to concentrate on Ethan's likes and dislikes. His life was recounted through an homage written by his parents. They projected photos of the day of his birth, his birthday parties with friends, family outings and a drawing he made shortly before he died. Balloons, flowers, tea candles and his favourite toys decorated the room and his casket. One cousin read a poem she wrote for him, a nurse recounted a favourite bedtime story and his sister and cousins made up a rap song about his life. At the end of the ceremony, two of his favourite clowns from the children's hospital led the mourners in a cortege to his gravesite. At the reception, Ethan's father observed that he could not have made it through the burial without the clowns' kind presence. His mother simply said: Ethan would have loved his funeral.

CONRAD

At the end of Conrad's funeral, his swimming team came to the front of the room and stood in a line in front of his coffin in a poignant moment of silence. Eight of them served as pallbearers. The rest of the team followed the coffin at a respectful distance, as they accompanied him to the cemetery.

JACQUELINE

Jacqueline died after a long full life. After the homage, some of her family members paid tribute to her through objects taken from her home. After speaking, they placed the object in a basket on the coffin and returned to their seat. One of Jacqueline's daughters held up a wooden spoon from her mother's kitchen and told of all the meals her mother had lovingly cooked for them with that worn old spoon. Her son showed a photo of his mother as a young woman in the prime of her life, and spoke of some of the memories that flooded back as he looked it. Her grandson opened his hand to reveal an object he had made in Scouts and given to his grandmother many years ago. He was touched that she had kept this simple gift for so many years.

NOAH

When Noah learned that he was terminally ill, he concentrated on doing what he could to ease his ten-year-old son Theo's transition into a life without him. As a single father, Noah's first concern was to name +a suitable carer for his son. Together they decided that Theo would live with Noah's sister Mira. Realizing that the funeral would be particularly tough for Theo, Noah prepared it carefully with a celebrant. A few months before he died, Noah and Theo moved in with Mira, her husband and their three children. During the ceremony, the celebrant read a letter Noah had written for Theo, expressing much gratitude for the time he been able to spend with his son. He also left Theo the watch he had received as a present from his own father.

ISABELLE

Isabelle died at the age of 64 after many years of illness. Her husband and their two adult daughters decided on cremation with a short intimate ceremony. A public funeral was held about two weeks later on a date that suited all of her family members. I helped them design and craft both ceremonies and then presided at the second.

On a small table at the front of the room, next to Isabelle's photo and urn, they placed flowers along with a cigarette and matches (symbols of freedom for Isabelle). Friends and family members paid their respects, each in their own way. The homage was written by her husband and daughters and read by an actress friend. Two friends, semi-professional singers, sang a moving piece of classical music. Her twin brother, elder sister and closest friend spoke about their relationship with Isabelle. A member of a volunteer organization she supported talked about her contributions to their work. One of her daughters wrote a text about her last exchange with her mother. Isabelle's philosophy of life came through in the last piece played at the ceremony: 'People have the power' by Patti Smith.

At the reception, there was food and drink but also a table laden with small objects, jewellery and scarves that had belonged to Isabelle. The family invited the 300 people present to choose whatever they wished as a keepsake. A month later, family members and Isabelle's closest friends were invited to the burial of her ashes on family land. A lilac, Isabelle's favourite flowering bush, was planted over her urn. Afterwards, they shared a picnic lunch to honour Isabelle's memory and to talk about the many happy meals they had shared with her at that same table.

CAROLINE

I first met Caroline in hospital at the request of her family. They asked me to support her as she faced yet another relapse in her illness. I quickly realized that Caroline had her own plan for me: she needed support to get her family – the people she loved most in the world – to accept her choice to stop treatment. Sorrowfully, they agreed to Caroline's decision to move back home with palliative care assistance. Over a period of ten days, the family laughed, cried and told stories, grateful for those last days together. Friends dropped for tea and to say goodbye. Caroline died as she wished, at home, in peace, surrounded by her family.

At the funeral, I read the homage that Caroline had written with her husband and children during those last days. It recalls the passion for life that fired Caroline's acts of love towards her neighbours – regardless of their race, culture or religion, her calm strength of character, her lucidity about her condition and her fearlessness in the face of death.

THE DURHAM FAMILY

Upon the passing of their most senior family member, a 96-year-old artist, his family got together to write down their complex history and update the family tree. They divided the homage into three 'acts' that represented three periods of his life. Each period was illustrated by a piece of his artwork, music and a story or tribute. At the close of the ceremony, the celebrant invited the mourners to file past the artist's paintings as they left the ceremonial space.

As a remembrance for future generations, the family put together a book composed of photos of the man and his artwork, the family tree, the homage, tributes and stories.

CHECKLIST FOR A FUNERAL CEREMONY

The bereaved need time to craft a bespoke ceremony. Count on taking five to ten days for the planning and creating phases. The ceremony itself is usually 30 to 40 minutes long. The time allotted by some funeral directors (15 to 20 minutes) is too short for most families. Longer ceremonies tend to be tiring for the bereaved.

Preparing your funeral spells out how to prepare a basic document for a funeral ceremony.

 Questionnaire on ritual identity. See the tool in Chapter 5.

 Five techniques for feeling safe should be used whenever needed during the grieving process.

PLANNING PHASE

Organizing a funeral is a heavy responsibility that should be shared whenever possible. Some things can only be done by legal representatives; other aspects can be delegated to those outside the deceased's inner circle. Opportunities for assisting the bereaved are as endless as their tasks.

Who?

The deceased is at the centre of the funeral (see Figure 10.1). Identify the crafting team very early on. Accompaniment by a professional is recommended.

 Prioritizing helps you determine who should participate in the funeral.

When? Where?

Take your time to decide what is suitable. Cremation has become popular in part because it gives the bereaved more freedom to meet their needs and those of their friends and relatives, particularly those who live at a distance.

⏸

PAUSE

CREATING PHASE

In this phase the craftspeople write texts and gather fitting elements for the ceremony. Use the most appropriate tools for your work together.

Core values is about the central values demonstrated by the life and relationships of the deceased.

Content

Homage and tributes

The homage or eulogy puts the deceased's life into focus, highlighting significant events and relationships in a chronological or thematic order. It is written from a neutral standpoint, usually by several family members and close friends, and read early in the ceremony. These points may be covered in a homage:

- Place and date of birth, full name (also name before marriage, if applicable)

- Childhood: family home, childhood friends and memories

- Education/vocational training: schools, internships, graduation, diplomas

- Family life: parents, siblings, godmother, godfather, marriage(s), children, grandchildren...

- Experience: professional, volunteer

- Interests: sports, hobbies, entertainment, reading, travel, art, languages, spirituality, knowledge of specialized fields

- Ties: family, close friendships

- Values, human qualities

- Stories, objects, sounds, taste that reflect who she or he was

- Death: date, place, location of 'final resting place'

The tribute is an act, a short speech, a piece of music or art that shows gratitude, respect or admiration for the deceased. Those doing tributes will most likely have been mentioned already in the homage. A short personal speech casts light on the deceased's relationships with one person or a group of people (friends, members of a club, work or volunteer context). Four to five tributes from people who represent different areas of the deceased's life round out a ceremony nicely.

Plumbing the meaning of core values may be helpful in writing a tribute around the identified themes or values.

Develop the idea into a short text or use it creatively to introduce a piece of music or a painting or sculpture or an object that reminds you of the deceased. Cultural psychologist Joanna Wojtkowiak (2017) encourages the bereaved to include the sensory and material dimension in ritualmaking.

Just the right music. See the tool in Chapter 5.

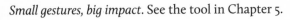

Small gestures, big impact. See the tool in Chapter 5.

Format

The order of ceremony should follow a logical pattern: welcome, homage, tributes, including musical tributes, letting go and closing. *Letting the deceased go is an essential part of a funeral.* It clearly, but kindly, states that the mourners have accomplished their duty to the deceased. As they leave the funeral area, they take their first steps without their loved one. If burial follows the ceremony, the letting go is pronounced near the end of the ceremony and enacted with symbolic gestures in the cemetery, where it may be hard to hear a speaker. These gestures of leave-taking – such as throwing dirt or flowers onto the coffin – vary from place to place and culture to culture.

 Format of the ceremony. See the tool in Chapter 5.

 Coherence test helps you finalize the choices made in the planning and creating phases.

PAUSE

REALIZING PHASE

The collective experience of the ceremony puts the mourners on the same page: everyone knows what the others know. This facilitates the grief process and encourages mutual support.

 Ritualizing, step by step. The setting should be as comfortable as possible for the bereaved. This includes the organization and overall timing of the funeral as well as a good sound system. If the celebrant or funeral director does not assume this role, make sure that someone does.

 Guidelines for readers. See the tool in Chapter 5.

Solace for the bereaved

Grief is not contagious but it elicits strong emotions that can feel like a malady. Mourners grieve in many different ways. Everyone needs to feel that their friends and family are there for them.

- Write a note to the family to tell them that you are thinking of them in their loss.
- Call or write in the days or weeks after the funeral to let your bereaved friend know that you are thinking of her or him.
- Propose a walk, music, a game or an activity you are used to doing together. Flexible, simple and spontaneous activities are often the best.
- Don't push her or him to talk, but don't avoid talking about loss either.
- Take her or him for a meal or for a coffee to show you have not forgotten.
- Don't be hurt, if there is no or little response. Be gently persistent.
- Send your friend a note or an email on the first anniversary to show you care about this important marker in her or his life.

RISK FACTORS AROUND FUNERALS

Getting it right is tough, especially in the case of a funeral for someone who dies suddenly or who leaves no instructions. There is little time for reflection and for tinkering until it feels right. Decisions fall basically into two categories: the permanent or irreversible and the ephemeral or reversible. Choosing whether or not to hold a public ceremony, and if there is one, what kind of ceremony, falls into the former category. Although many of my colleagues and I have 'redone' faulty ceremonies, years of pain and sorrow often go by before a more fitting tribute is performed. A living will[2] contributes to resting in peace.

The greatest risk for you, as a bereaved person, if you decide to preside the ceremony of a close friend or relative, is that your own grief process may be stalled. You are at the service of others and cannot be attentive to your own needs.

---

2   In most countries, people can make a legal document that specifies what actions should be taken by whom as regards their health if, for any reason, they are no longer able to make decisions for themselves. In the US, it has a legal status and may also cover funeral arrangements. In France, the family can be fined or jailed if the deceased's wishes for the funeral are not respected.

CHECKLIST FOR RITUALIZING IN PUBLIC SPACES

PLANNING
First things first

☐ We are clear about our objectives for this event

We have identified:

☐ **About?** Who or what is at the centre of ritualization

☐ **By whom?** Who is **responsible for crafting/organizing/presiding**

☐ **With whom?** Who participates/is invited

☐ **What?** Define the occasion

☐ **When?** Determine **date/time/duration**

☐ **Where?** Choose **place/setting/venue**

COMMUNICATION AND CONTINGENCY

☐ We have contacted or invited all ('With whom?') noted above

☐ Participants have approved their roles

☐ If there is disagreement about how to proceed we know who makes the final decision

☐ We have contingency plans and leeway for timing

PAUSE

CREATING
Making sense (craftspeople)

We, the craftspeople, are agreed on:

☐ **Why and how** we ritualize this event/situation

☐ What is at the **HEART ♥** of the event/situation

☐ The **key values, ideals or philosophy of life** we wish to convey

☐ **Decisions confirmed** (Who, What, When, Where)

☐ If there is disagreement, we have discussed the issues

CONTENT

☐ **Words** that express what is at the ♥

☐ **Music/gestures/symbols/objects**

FORMAT

☐ Is **coherent** with kind of event/situation

☐ **Social gathering**

☐ **Reminder list**

☐ If necessary, **we have tested our plan**

PAUSE

REALIZING
Expressing meaning

☐ **Prepare setting** (participants/presider)

☐ **Open event** (presider)

☐ **Ritualizing** (Content + Format)

☐ **Leadership coherent** with kind of event/situation

☐ **Close formal part** (presider)

☐ **Social gathering** (all)

☐ **Close event and clean up** (organizer)

DURATION OF EVENT (suggested)

Ceremony (to be determined)

Social gathering (to be determined)

April 2016. This checklist is not intended to be comprehensive. Modifications to fit specific situations are encouraged.

ASHOKA

RITUALIZING IN PUBLIC SPACES

Rites, no matter how sacred, are assessed, judged wanting or judged adequate...humans evaluate and criticize everything, ritual included.

Ronald L. Grimes (2004, p.339)

Art-filled ritual practices address and satisfy evolved needs of human psychology. They create and reinforce emotionally reassuring and psychologically necessary feelings of close relationship with others and of belonging to a group. Further, they provide to individuals a sense of meaningfulness or cognitive order and individual competence insofar as they give emotional force to explanations of how the world came to be as it is and what is required to maintain it. They are adaptive not only because they join people together in common cause but because they also relieve anxiety. It is better to have something to do, with others, in times of uncertainty rather than try to cope by oneself or do nothing at all.

Ellen Dissanayake (2016)

Remote from rationality, [the] finality [of ritual] remains fundamentally emotional and communal; the good of the species is at stake!

Matthieu Smyth (2017)

Whereas the previous chapters of this book deal with how to ritualize our own major and minor life events, this chapter tackles how to go about crafting ritual in public places for people outside our inner circles.

As ritual paradigms shift, expectations for ceremonies in public spaces[1] rise: they, too, must be and feel right. Our need to 'do something' – play, make art and ritualize – is a natural response to the challenges of life and death. Yet, just as 'art for art's sake' does not work, ritual for ritual's sake is not effective either. Contemporary public rituals that have missed the mark include corruption-riddled sport competitions that attract headlines such as 'Corruption in sport: Market-driven morality' (Chadwick 2013). Music award ceremonies draw fire too: 'At last: The classic BRIT awards exposed as a sickening crime against classical music' (Morely 2012, p.265). Meaning is challenged and emotion runs high: play is not about power. Making art is not about consumer culture. Ritualizing is not about the sponsors of an event.

I recently attended a graduation ceremony where one-third of the students chosen for special awards were absent. Mentally, I went through my checklist for ritualizing and observed that the significance of the graduates' accomplishments was not at the heart of the ritual. The multi-media and dance presentations, the assembly gathered, and the graduates themselves were accessories to an event that proclaimed 'look what the system did!' The heart of the occasion could have been acknowledged, if a few of the graduates had spoken about what their accomplishments meant to them as future professionals in an uncertain world.

When official events are consistently off the mark, marginal events – such as protest marches, ephemeral memorials for the dead, occupying a building, a square or a *terrain vague*[2] – surface to denounce corruption, poverty, rampant consumerism, the dangers of global surveillance, and social, racial and economic inequities. Notable events include Occupy

---

1   The term 'public space' generally refers to an area that is open and accessible to people for transport as well as for economic and social interaction: roads, the pavement, and where it has been expanded into squares, as well as small grassy or abandoned areas, open marketplaces, farmers' markets, public commons, public greens and piers.

2   *Terrain vague* is a French term that means 'empty lot' or 'space'. Architect and philosopher Ignasi de Solà-Morales used the term in the 1990s, applying it to abandoned, obsolete and unproductive areas with no clear definitions and limits. Since then it has been used by scholars and urbanists alike, to talk about the problematic and potential value of vacant lots, railroad tracks and other marginal urban spaces. See Sassen (2001) and Mariani and Barron (2014).

Wall Street in New York City and *Nuit Debout* (Up All Night), which began in Paris before spreading to other cities in France. Sociologist Saskia Sassen says: The 'global street' (2011)[3] is 'an indeterminate space where the powerless[4] can be makers' (Sassen and Thompson 2014). '[It contributes to constituting] a public domain via ritualization… Powerlessness is not simply an absolute status that can be flattened into the absence of power… It contains the possibility of making the political, the civic, a history' (Sassen 2013, p.213). The ritualization of protest in public spaces takes many forms: one group publicly questions consumer culture values and encourages the search for viable solutions (see 'The Story of Stuff') while another draws attention to the plight of Indigenous women (see 'Walking with our sisters').

In reaction to across-the-board budget cuts in education, health and culture in Geneva, thousands of people (myself included) occupied the streets with placards. Mine was marked, 'You think culture is expensive? Try ignorance!' Officials passed the budget without a nod to our concerns. In true Swiss style, we hit the streets again – this time to collect signatures for a referendum. Genevan voters decided the issue in June 2016 – over 60 per cent of those voting refused the budget cuts. Even if our efforts to stop the cuts had been unsuccessful, our protest – like those mentioned above – would have still marked our desire to 'do something' in public space about the world we live in and the heritage we leave to our children. We wrote our own history.

---

3   Sassen notes that the 'global street' is shrinking 'due to the financial crisis'. Powerful actors buy up urban land and buildings as investments, which leads to the expulsion of those who can't pay. 'Their logic becomes the logic of development. And we – the citizens – lose rights…[as] the spaces for the powerless in cities shrink. You know, this whole notion that I have about the powerless being able to make history in cities – that doesn't happen in an office park' (Sassen 2014).

4   The kind of powerlessness associated with trauma cannot be considered a base for action. Traumatized people in particular need the strength of the group for ritualizing in public spaces (see Chapter 2).

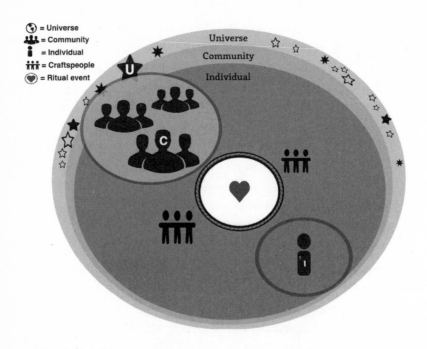

Figure 11.1. Ritualizing in public spaces
The creation phase is just as crucial in the ritualization of events in public places as it is
in the celebration of life events. The craftspeople determine what is at the heart of the
occasion. Public ritualizing makes sense, is coherent and authentic when every aspect
of the ritualmaking – including the different actors, their relationships and the broader
context – reflects this 'heart'.

EIGHT SITUATIONS

MOVING HOUSE

Imke van Dillen works to relieve tension in Dutch society by ritualizing
events around the destruction of family homes that must be pulled down
to make way for multi-family buildings. She brings together people with
different interests and levels of investment – home dwellers, real estate
agents, builders, representatives from the town hall – to craft fitting rituals
that say goodbye to a beloved place and open the way for new housing.

WALKING WITH OUR SISTERS

Over the last 30 years some 1181 First Nations women and girls in Canada were murdered or reported missing. People who want to draw attention to this injustice created a commemorative installation. It is made up of 1763+ pairs of beaded moccasin vamps (tops) plus 108 pairs of children's vamps. Each pair of vamps represents one missing or murdered Indigenous woman or one child who never returned home from a residential school. The moccasins are left unfinished to represent the unfinished lives of these sisters, mothers, aunties, daughters, cousins, grandmothers, wives and partners.

Visitors to this floor installation remove their shoes to walk on a winding fabric path through the pairs of vamps and scattered cedar boughs. These women's lives were cut short; they have gone missing but they are not forgotten.[5]

GHOST BIKES

When there is a violent death, a terrorist attack or a well-known person dies, memorials spring up on the spot or nearby to honour the dead. The memorials are most often created by unidentified people.

> Ghost bikes are small and sombre memorials for bicyclists who are killed or hit on the street. A bicycle is painted all white and locked to a street sign near the crash site, accompanied by a small plaque. They serve as reminders of the tragedy that took place on an otherwise anonymous street corner, and as quiet statements in support of cyclists' right to safe travel. The first ghost bikes were created in St. Louis, Missouri in 2003. Currently there are over 630 ghost bikes that have since appeared in over 210 locations throughout the world.[6]

5   See http://walkingwithoursisters.ca
6   Taken from http://ghostbikes.org

THE STORY OF STUFF

'Making art is better than shopping' is a reminder that we have more power to make our world better as citizens than as shoppers. Annie Leonard spent almost three decades investigating where our 'stuff' comes from and where it goes when we throw it away. About ten years ago, she and her friends put a 20-minute movie about her findings on the internet. It channelled concern about the impact of consumer culture values on people and the planet, and it encourages protest against consumer culture values by searching for solutions.

Destiny Watford and her friends in Baltimore used art, poetry and powerful, informed testimony to get their school board to divest from a polluting incinerator energy producer to a solar farm project. Wendy Gordon and David Sand launched the PIPs Rewards[7] mobile app to steer people towards a marketplace where they can earn PIPs by making healthy choices about transport, buying used clothing and books, and recycling electronics; they can spend PIPs at organic food stores or by micro-investing in community solar projects. Edmond and his wife Janet started one of Hong Kong's first urban farm-to-table restaurants.

PEACE LANTERN CEREMONY

On 6 August 1945, the US dropped an atomic bomb on the Japanese city of Hiroshima. Three days later, the city of Nagasaki suffered the same fate. The bombs are credited with bringing an end to the Second World War, but up to 200,000 civilians died. Those who lived were wounded, maimed and suffered atrocious pain. The two blasts represent the only wartime use of nuclear weapons on a civilian population.

The 70th anniversary of the bombings was commemorated, on 6 August 2015, with the ageing survivors. Every year on this date, thousands of people gather at the Motoyasu river bank in Hiroshima Peace Park to participate in the floating lantern peace ceremony.

---

7   PIPs are Positive Impact Points. Rewards you earn when you do good things, make healthy choices and shop more responsibly. http://pipsrewards.com

PEACEMAKING CIRCLES

Many schools in poor urban areas in the US see their students follow what is known as the school-to-prison pipeline. In Oakland, California, one of the most violent cities in the nation, schools have adopted a programme with 'restorative justice circles'. These circles give a framework for respectful discussions with and among troubled youth. Each person holds a special object to show it is his or her turn to speak. Teachers, parents, friends or members of the school administration stop and sit down together to talk about the problems they face. The others listen, give their perspective and try to find solutions that support all concerned. Through these ritualized peacemaking circles long-time enemies have become friends and suspensions and racial disparity in discipline have decreased. More students with failing grades and multiple incarcerations are finishing school, some of them quite successfully (Davis 2015).

TRAUMA AND TRIUMPH

The South African Truth and Reconciliation Commission (TRC) was an official body that served from 1995 to 2003 to ease the transition into a new era. As a modern performance ritual, it set the stage for a new national narrative. Like threads, the testimonies given to the TRC were woven into this drama of trauma and triumph. As people were able to tell their stories, they began to deal with the disaster, both natural and human, of apartheid, and to move through this major transition (Goodman 2006).

NAMES AND NUMBERS

Ritual artist Ida van der Lee creates participative rituals in parks, squares and graveyards in the Netherlands. In one project that Ida calls 'Names and Numbers', she and her team help survivors – and Dutch society as a whole – deal with the sadness and residual guilt from the deportation of thousands of Dutch Jews during the Second World War. In a public square in Amsterdam, near the Jewish quarter, people are invited to choose the name of a deported person who died in exile, write the name on a plaque, ring a bell, speak the person's name and place the plaque on a grid.

Figure 11.2. Names and numbers, Amsterdam, Netherlands
This 4 May participative commemoration for Jews forcibly expelled from the
Netherlands during the Second World War will take place every year until there
is a name plaque for each deportee.
© Ida van der Lee

CHECKLIST FOR RITUALIZING
IN PUBLIC SPACES

Most organizers are brilliant in planning and realizing an event. Many fail
to include the creation phase when making emerging rituals. These three
tools tease out the heart of the occasion and ensure that it is coherent
with the elements of the event.

 Why and how? See the tool in Chapter 5.

 Core values. See the tool in Chapter 5.

 Coherence test. See the tool in Chapter 5.

RISK FACTORS FOR RITUALIZING IN PUBLIC SPACES

The main risk for the event lies in a ritualization that misses the point. As citizens who accept incoherent and inauthentic public ritualization, the main risk is that others will write our history, decide for us now, and make our future.

The situations described above represent new ways of ritualizing in public spaces.

CONCLUSION

We are at the cusp of an ultra-modern era of change that challenges each one of us to redefine our identity. As villages and parishes give way to megalopolis and personalized communities, ritual practice remains 'the rhyme and rhythm of society' (Hall and Ames 1998, p.270). Life events can be 'liked' but not marked on Facebook. Virtual communication cannot replace face-to-face encounters. Ritualizing our relationships requires care, time and intentional effort.

I began this book by observing that when I realized liturgical rites no longer satisfied my need for ritual, I started to explore how to mark important events without religion. As I intuitively crafted personalized ceremonies for weddings and funerals, I felt the power of secular ritual to bring people together and make the ordinary *extra*-ordinary. I wondered whether what works for me might be useful for others. This book presents my approach to creating ritual and how to use it; I hope that it is useful to you.

Ritual that obeys the highest laws is respectful of people, relationships and the world; as such it represents a profoundly humanizing and civilizing activity that firmly anchors us in a new reality. Meaningful ritual is based on appropriate content and is conducted by the right people for the right people/relationship/event in a fitting context. Ritual is not a game but it can be playful; it is not therapy but it can be therapeutic; it is not theatre but it is theatrical; it is not art, but it is artistic. Above all, it must make sense and be coherent with the values and objectives of whomever or whatever is at the centre of the ritualization.

Crafting secular ritual can help us preserve, or reinstate, healthy rhythms in our lives and in society as a whole, as well as reinforce the natural rhythms of our planet. The ideal effect of ritual on the individual is a sense of ease, security and belonging (Sung 2012; Heinskou and Liebst

2016). When we get together – physically – to ritualize our joys, concerns and sorrows, we feel less alone, more supported, inventive, proactive, safe and alive. Through ritual we can constructively and peacefully resist dehumanization by reclaiming time in our busy lives for relationships, divesting ourselves of the desire for stuff and taking our rightful place in public spaces. Like the ancients, we too can harness the power of ritual to heal ourselves, our community and our universe, and make our own history.

REFERENCES

Allemand Smaller, A. (2017: in press) 'Multicultural Wedding Ceremonies. Venturing into the World of Diversity.' In J. Gordon-Lennox, *Emerging Ritual in Secular Societies: A Transdisciplinary Conversation*: Jessica Kingsley Publishers.

Allison, D.G. (1996) *Two or Three Things I Know for Sure*. London: Penguin Books.

Artigas, L. and Jarero, I. (1998) 'The Butterfly Hug Method for Bilateral Stimulation.' Available at http://emdrresearchfoundation.org/toolkit/butterfly-hug.pdf, accessed on 14 February 2016.

Asad, T. (1993) *Genealogies of Religion: Discipline and Reasons of Power in Christianity and Islam*. Baltimore, MD: Johns Hopkins University Press.

Asad, T. (2003) *Formations of the Secular: Christianity, Islam, Modernity.* Cultural Memory in the Present Series. Stanford, CA: Stanford University Press.

Bacqué, M.F. (2010) 'Avoir moins peur de la vie et de la mort.' *Psychologies.com.* Available at www.psychologies.com/Moi/Epreuves/Deuil/Articles-et-Dossiers/Avoir-moins-peur-de-la-vie-et-de-la-mort/Marie-Frederique-Bacque-L-absence-de-rites-accroit-la-peur/L-appauvrissement-des-rites-serait-donc-source-de-complications-psychologiques, accessed on 19 August 2010.

Bell, C. (1997) *Ritual: Perspectives and Dimensions*. New York: Oxford University Press. Aslan, R. in OUP prefaced edition, 2009.

Bell, C. (no date) *Believing and the Practice of Religion*. Unpublished manuscript, Santa Clara University Library.

Brown, R.M. (1988) 'Introduction.' *Starting from Scratch*. New York: Bantam Books.

Chadwick, S. (2013) 'Corruption in sport: Market-driven morality.' *The Economist* 22 April. Available at www.economist.com/blogs/gametheory/2013/04/corruption-sport-0, accessed on 18 April 2016.

Chang, S.T. (1986) *The Complete System of Self-Healing. Internal Exercises*. San Francisco, CA: Tao Publishing.

Chopra, M. (2014) *100 Promises for My Child*. London: Profile Books.

Damasio, A. (2003) *Looking for Spinoza: Joy, Sorrow and the Feeling Brain*. New York: Harcourt Books.

Damasio, A. and Damasio H. (2006–present) Brain and Creativity Institute. Feelings Program. Available at http://dornsife.usc.edu/bci/feelings-program, accessed on 13 February 2016.

Davis, F. (2015) 'Heal Don't Punish.' In S. van Gelder and staff, *Sustainable Happiness*. Oakland, CA: Berrett-Koehler Publishers.

de Haan, T. (2015) Available at http://tiudehaan.com/ceremony, accessed on 12 December 2015.

Dissanayake, E. (1992) *Homo Aestheticus: Where Art Comes From and Why*. New York: Free Press.

Dissanayake, E. (2000) *Art and Intimacy: How the Arts Began*. Seattle, WA: University of Washington Press.

Dissanayake, E. (2002) *What is Art For?* Seattle, WA: University of Washington Press (original published 1988).

Dissanayake, E. (2004) 'The Art of Ritual and the Ritual of Art.' In Penland School of Crafts (ed.) *The Nature of Craft and the Penland Experience*. Penland, NC: Lark Books.

Dissanayake, E. (2007) Interview: 'A Conversation about Art and Biology with Ellen Dissanayake by Steury, T.' Washington State University, Available at http://wsm.wsu.edu/s/we.php?id=206, accessed on 15 April 2016.

Dissanayake, E. (2009) 'Bodies Swayed to Music: The Temporal Arts as Integral to Ceremonial Ritual.' In S. Malloch and C. Trevarthen (eds) *Communicative Musicality* (pp. 533–544). Oxford: Oxford University Press.

Dissanayake, E. (2016) Personal communication.

Eco, U. (2009) 'We Like Lists Because We Don't Want to Die.' Interview by S. Beyer and L. Gorris. In *Spiegel*. 11 November 2009. Available at www.spiegel.de/international/zeitgeist/spiegel-interview-with-umberto-eco-we-like-lists-because-we-don-t-want-to-die-a-659577.html, accessed on 25 January 2016.

Economist, The (2010) 'Age and happiness: The U-bend of life: Why, beyond middle age, people get happier as they get older.' 16 December. Available at www.economist.com/node/17722567, accessed on 8 March 2016.

Fields, J. (2011–15) Good Life Project Living Creed 2.0. Available at www.goodlifeproject.com/creed, accessed on 9 February 2016.

Gairin, V. (2010) 'Nouveaux rites.' Dossier Pensez la mort, *Le Point*. Mai-Juin.

Gawande, A. (2011) *The Checklist Manifesto: How to Get Things Right*. New York: Picador Press.

Ghostbikes.org. Available at www.ghostbikes.org, accessed on 12 March 2016.

Goodman, T. (2006) 'Performing a "New" Nation: The Role of the TRC in South Africa.' In J.C. Alexander, B. Giesen and J.L. Mast (eds) *Social Performance. Symbolic Action, Cultural Pragmatics and Ritual* (pp.169–92). New York: Cambridge University Press.

Grand, D. (2013) *Brainspotting: The Revolutionary New Therapy for Rapid and Effective Change*. Boulder, CO: True Sounds.

Grimes, R.L. (2016) Personal correspondence.

Grimes, R.L. (2004) cited by Hüskens, U. (2007) 'Ritual Dynamics and Ritual Failure.' In U. Hüskens (ed.) *When Rituals Go Wrong: Mistakes, Failure, and the Dynamics of Ritual*. Leiden and Boston: Brill.

Grimes, R.L. (2002) *Deeply into the Bone, Re-Inventing Rites of Passage*. London: University of California Press (first edition 2000).

Hall, D.L. and Ames, R.T. (1998) *Thinking from the Han: Self, Truth, and Transcendence in Chinese and Western Culture*. Albany, NY: State University of New York Press.

Heinskou, M.B. and Liebst, L.S. (2016) 'On the elementary neural forms of micro-interactional rituals: Integrating autonomic nervous system functioning into interaction ritual theory.' *Sociological Forum*. 31.1.

Holloway, M. (2015) 'Ritual and Meaning-Making in the Face of Contemporary Death.' Keynote lecture Symposium: Emerging Rituals in a Transitioning Society. Utrecht: University of Humanistic Studies.

ICM Research on behalf of Co-operative Funeralcare (2010) 'The Ways We Say Goodbye.' Reported in British Religion in Numbers. Available at www.brin.ac.uk/2011/the-ways-we-say-goodbye, accessed on 1 March 2016.

IEP (Internet Encyclopedia of Philosophy) (no date) 'Xunzi.' Available at www.iep.utm.edu/xunzi/, accessed on 7 February 2016.

Illich, I. (1973) *Tools for Conviviality*. New York: Harper & Row.

Jonte-Pace, D. (2009) 'Foreword.' In OUP prefaced edition of C. Bell, *Ritual Theory, Ritual Practice*. New York: Oxford University Press (originally published in 1992).

Katz, R. (1982) *Boiling Energy: Community Healing Among the Kalahari !Kung*. Cambridge, MA: Harvard University Press.

Kline III, T.C. (2004) 'Moral cultivation through ritual participation: Xunzi's philosophy of ritual.' In K. Schilbrack (ed.) *Thinking Through Rituals*. New York: Routledge.

Kuhn, T. (1996 [1962]) *The Structure of Scientific Revolution*. Chicago, IL: University of Chicago Press (originally published 1962).

Leonard, A. (2008–present) 'The Story of Stuff Project.' Available at http://storyofstuff.org, accessed on 7 February 2016.

Lenoir, F. (2012) *La Guérison du monde*. Paris: Fayard (author's translation).

Levine, P.A. (2005) 'Foreword.' In M. Picucci, *Ritual as Resource: Energy for Vibrant Living*. Berkeley, CA: North Atlantic Books.

Levine, P.A. (2010) *In an Unspoken Voice*. Berkeley, CA: North Atlantic Books.

Levine, P.A. (2015) *Trauma and Memory: Brain and Body in a Search for the Living Past: A Practical Guide for Understanding and Working with Traumatic Memory*. Berkeley, CA: North Atlantic Books.

Mariani, M. and Barron, P. (eds) (2014) *Terrain Vague. Interstices at the Edge of the Pale*. New York: Routledge.

Mies van der Rohe, L. (1938) Inaugural address as Director of Architecture at the Armour Institute of Technology, Chicago, IL, 20 November. In Papers of Ludwig Mies van der Rohe, Box 61. Manuscript Division, Library of Congress.

Mies van der Rohe, L. (2010) Cited in G.P. Borden, 'Preface', *Material Precedent. Typology of Modern Tectonics*. Hoboken, NJ: John Wiley & Sons, Inc.

Morely, P. cited in Rhodes, J. (2014) *Instrumental*. Edinburgh: Canongate.tv.

My Climate.org. Website for calculating carbon imprint. Available at www.myclimate.org, accessed on 15 December 2015.

Myerhoff, B. G. (1999) cited in E.M. Broner, *Bringing Home the Light: A Jewish Woman's Handbook of Rituals*. San Francisco, CA: Council Oak Books.

National Funeral Directors Association (NFDA) Report (2015) cited in Davis, S. 'How secular Americans are reshaping funeral rituals.' Religious News Service, 17 December 2015. Available at www.religionnews.com/2015/12/17/nonreligious-reshaping-american-burial-rituals/, accessed on 1 March 2016.

Neiman, S. (2014) *Why Grow Up? Subversive Thoughts for an Infantile Age*. New York: Farrar, Straus & Giroux.

Odate, T. (1998) *Japanese Woodworking Tools: Their Tradition, Spirit and Use*. Fresno, CA: Linden Publishing Inc. (originally published 1984).

Panksepp, J. and Biven, L. (2012) *The Archeology of the Mind: Neuroevolutionary Origins of Human Emotion*. New York: W.W. Norton & Company.

People's Paths, The (1993) Declaration of War Against Exploiters of Lakota Spirituality. Available at www.thepeoplespaths.net, accessed on 28 October 2015.

Pew Research Center (2015a) 'The Future of World Religions: Population Growth Projections, 2010–2050.' 2 April. Available at www.pewforum.org/2015/04/02/religious-projections-2010-2050/#fn-22652-5, accessed on 25 November 2015.

Pew Research Center (2015b) 'Statistics of Unaffiliated Population by Region, 2010 and 2050.' Available at www.pewforum.org/2015/04/02/religiously-unaffiliated/pf_15-04-02_projectionstables82b, accessed on 2 April 2015.

Picucci, M. (2005) *Ritual as Resource: Energy for Vibrant Living.* Berkeley, CA: North Atlantic Books.

Porges, S.W. (2011) *The Polyvagal Theory: Neurophysiological Foundations of Emotions, Attachment, Communication and Self-Regulation.* New York: W.W. Norton & Company.

Porges, S.W. (2012) Interview with William Stranger at Dharma Cafe. 6 June 2012. Available at https://vimeo.com/44146020, accessed on 3 February 2016.

Sassen, S. (2001) *The Global City.* Princeton, NJ: Princeton University Press.

Sassen, S. (2011) 'The Global Street: Making the Political.' *Globalizations 8*, 5, 573–579. Available at http://dx.doi.org/10.1080/14747731.2011.622458, accessed on 16 December 2015.

Sassen, S. (2013) 'Does the City Have Speech?' In T. Haas and K. Olsson (eds) *Emergent Urbanism: Urban Planning and Design in Times of Structural and Systemic Change* (pp.209–222). Burlington, VT, USA and Farnham, UK: Ashgate Publishing.

Sassen, S. (2014) Interview by A. Dharssi, 'Cities are places where the powerless can shape history: the Right to the City in the 21st century.' *The Global Urbanist.* 13 December. Available at http://globalurbanist.com/2014/12/03/saskia-sassen-right-to-the-city, accessed on 12 March 2016.

Sassen, S. and Thompson, N. (2014) 'Saskia Sassen Talks Finance, Climate, Race, Immigration and How We Can Begin to Fix Our Planet.' In CreativeTime Reports. Available at http://creativetimereports.org/2014/10/27/saskia-sassen-finance-climate-race-immigration-creative-time-summit, accessed on 20 January 2016.

Scaer, R.C. (2006) 'The Precarious Present.' *Psychotherapy Networker 30*, 6, 49–53, 67.

Scaer, R.C. (2012) *8 Keys to Body–Brain Balance.* New York: W.W. Norton & Company.

Scaer, R.C. (2017: in press) 'The Neurophysiology of Ritual and Trauma: Cultural Implications.' In J. Gordon-Lennox, *Emerging Ritual in Secular Societies: A Transdisciplinary Conversation.* London: Jessica Kingsley Publishers.

Schirch, L. (2005) *Ritual and Symbol in Peacebuilding.* Bloomfield, CT: Kumarian Press.

Schnarch, D.M. (1997) *Passionate Marriage: Love, Sex, and Intimacy in Emotionally Committed Relationships.* New York: W.W. Norton & Company.

Seligman, A.B, Weller, R.P., Puett, M. and Simon, B. (2008) *Ritual and Its Consequences: An Essay on the Limits of Sincerity.* New York: Oxford Press.

Serra, A. (1996) *Nathan Never 59.* Milan, Italy: Sergio Bonelli Editore.

Smyth, M. (2011–2016) Private communications.

Smyth, M. (2017: in press) 'Human Rituals and Ethology: A Scholarly Journey.' In J. Gordon-Lennox, *Emerging Ritual in Secular Societies: A Transdisciplinary Conversation.* London: Jessica Kingsley Publishers.

Steinem, G. (2012) 'How I Got into this Room.' *The Humanist.* 18 October. Available at http://thehumanist.com/magazine/november-december-2012/features/how-i-got-into-this-room, accessed on 27 June 2016.

Stolz, J. and Könemann, J. (2011) Swiss National Research Programme. PNR 58.

Sung, W. (2012) 'Ritual in the Xunzi: A Change of the Heart/Mind.' *Sophia 51*, 2, 211–226.

SunLife (2015) 'Cost of Dying 2015.' Report posted 9 October 2015. Available at www. sunlifedirect.co.uk/press-office/cost-of-dying-2015/, accessed on 1 March 2016.

Sutherland, S. (2012) 'Ritual Science.' *Spirituality & Health*, September–October. Available at http://spiritualityhealth.com/articles/ritual-science?page=0%2C0, accessed on 14 March 2015.

Tavor, O. (2013) 'Xunzi's Theory of Ritual Revisited: Reading Ritual as Corporal Technology.' *Dao: A Journal of Comparative Philosophy 12*, 3, 313–30.

Tomatis, A.A. (1988) *Les Troubles Scolaires.* Paris: Ergo Press.

Ueland, B. (1938 [2010]) *If You Want to Write.* New York: BN Publishing (originally published 1938).

van der Kolk, B.A. (2011) 'Foreword.' In S.W. Porges, *The Polyvagal Theory: Neurophysiological Foundations of Emotions, Attachment, Communication and Self-Regulation.* New York: W.W. Norton & Company.

van der Kolk, B.A. (2014) *The Body Keeps the Score. Brain, Mind, and Body in the Healing of Trauma.* New York: Viking Books.

van der Kolk, B.A. (2015) 'Foreword.' In P.A. Levine, *Trauma and Memory: Brain and Body in a Search for the Living Past: A Practical Guide for Understanding and Working with Traumatic Memory.* Berkeley, CA: North Atlantic Books.

van Gelder, S. and Yes! staff (2014) *Sustainable Happiness.* Oakland, CA: Berrett-Koehler Publishers.

van Gennep, A. (1909) *Les Rites de Passage.* Paris: Librairie Stock.

Walkingwithoursisters.ca (2016) A Commemorative Art Installation for the Missing and Murdered Indigenous Women of Canada and the United States. Available at http://walkingwithoursisters.ca/about, accessed on 28 April 2016.

Watson, B. (1964) translator. *Hsün Tzu, Basic Writings.* New York: Columbia University Press.

Wojtkowiak, J. (2017: in press) 'Sensing the Dead: The Role of Embodiment, the Senses and Material Objects in the Realization of Mourning.' In J. Gordon-Lennox, *Emerging Ritual in Secular Societies: A Transdisciplinary Conversation.* London: Jessica Kingsley Publishers.

INDEX

Page numbers followed by lower case *f*, *t*, *c*, and *n* indicate *figures, tables, checklists and footnotes, respectively.*

Achebe, Chinua 58–9n2
activism *see* public space rituals
adoption 100
aesthetics 58, 79
affecting presence 58
African tribal rituals 22–3
aging and milestone transitions
  childhood dream fulfillment 135–6
  Confucian philosophy on 131
  growing up celebrations 134
  and happiness 131–2
  menstruation workshops 134
  retirement 79, 83, 84, 85, 136
  ritual planning celebrating 130c, 133f, 137
  see also birthdays; coming of age events
alcohol 62
aliveness 38, 164
Allemand Smaller, A. 129n3
Allison, D. 43
Alternative identities 28f, 29, 30n5, 90
Ames, R.T. 19, 19n1, 163
Analects (Confucius) 131
ancient ritual practices 22–3, 30, 31–3
anniversaries
  commemoration rituals 46f, 156–7, 158
  grief support on death 150
  wedding 79, 83, 84, 85, 132
  see also birthdays
anxiety 24, 38–9n8, 69–71, 153
apartheid performance rituals 159
art 22, 24, 50–1, 58, 59
Artigas, L. 70
artisans, amateur 42–3, 76t
Asad, T. 25, 26
atomic bomb commemorations 158
attunement
  aging and 131
  group ritualization for 35
  for identity formation 24
  modern civilization and need for 33–4
  mother-child interactions for 23
  as ritual purpose and benefit 23–4, 35–6, 62
Australia 118, 118n1
authenticity
  core values identification and
    expression for 78–80, 80–1t
  gestures and symbols selected for 84–5
  for meaningfulness 43, 51–2

  non-religious options and expectation of 140
  as ritualmaking goal 19, 61

Bacqué, M.F. 141
balloons 49
baptisms 54, 55, 84, 96–7
Barron, P. 154n2
Bauhaus 50–1, 59
Bell, C. 18, 24, 25, 27
belonging 24, 27–8, 56, 153, 163
BH (butterfly hugs) 69–70
bicyclists memorials 157
Bilateral Stimulation (BLS)
  techniques 35n6, 69–70, 72
birthdays
  as coming of age events 109–10, 112–13
  examples of 133–4, 135–6, 136
  function and significance of 131–3, 133f
  naming ceremony guest book
    traditions for 98–9
  planning and implementation
    steps for 130c, 137
  as welcoming ceremonies 99–100
bittersweetness 47, 62, 117
Biven, Lucy 23n2
BLS (Bilateral Stimulation)
  techniques 35n6, 69–70, 72
Borden, G.P. 50
Brain and Creativity Institute 34n5
BRIT awards 154
Broner, E.M. 62
Brown, R.M. 62
Buddhist traditions 28, 37, 100, 229
butterfly hugs (BH) 69–70

Canada 118, 118n1, 156–7
carbon imprints 48
celebrants, professional 20, 75–6, 76t, 118, 140
central person 55–6, 55f, 74, 76t, 78–9
ceremonies (realizing phase)
  aesthetics and affecting presence of 58
  choreography and format planning 85–7
  closure 88
  content of, as design component 56
  creative process phase descriptions
    and symbolism 62
  opening 87
  reader guidelines 88–9

risk factors for 62
setting up and preparation 87
socializing transition 88
troubleshooting during 87
see also specific types of ceremonies
Chang, S.T. 72
Chadwick, S. 154
checklists
    benefits of 64–5, 66
    for coming of age events 106*c*
    functions of 65
    for funeral ceremonies 138*c*
    for growing up rituals 130*c*
    for naming ceremonies 92*c*
    purpose of 65
    read-do style of 65
    risk factors with 66
    for public space rituals 152*c*
    for wedding ceremonies 116*c*
childhood dream fulfillment 135–6
children
    adopted 100
    attention spans of 83, 102
    birthday celebrations 109–10, 112–13, 133–4
    childrearing conditions and rights of 93–4
    circumcision rites 98
    confidence-building accomplishments 134
    with disabilities 99–100, 111, 125
    end of mothering rituals and adult 111–12
    funerals for 142–3
    happiness instruction 132
    mother-child bonding behaviours 23
    parent deaths and funeral planning for 143–4
    stepfamily cohesion rituals 135
    venue accessibility and 102–3, 125
    voice frequencies of 71
    see also coming of age events;
        naming ceremonies
Chopra, M. 101
choreography 85–7 104
circumcision rites 98
civic/social events 79, 83, 85
coherence 30, 36*f*, 57, 82, 83*t*
coming of age events
    examples of 109–13
    function and significance of 107–8
    gestures and symbols for 84
    planning and implementation 106*c*, 113–15
    risk factors 115
    role diagrams for 109*f*
    weddings in history as 117
commemoration rituals 46*f*, 156–7, 158
communication 54, 61, 65, 131n1, 163
competence 56, 153
compromise 74
confidence 35, 134
Confucianism 31–3, 37, 131
consumer culture protests 157–8
content 36*f*, 56, 126

context 27*f*, 36*f*, 54–5
cooperation 47, 105
CRAFTS (Create, Respect, Aesthetics,
    Form, Truth, Simplicity) 57–60
craftspeople
    amateur artisan 42–3, 76*t*
    professional celebrants 20, 75–6, 118, 140
    requirements of 43
    as ritual material 53
    role identification and assignment 55–6, 55*f*
    tools for 65–6
creativity 36, 50–1, 51*f*, 132
croning ceremonies 57
cultural appropriation 43–4, 115

Damasio, A. 34–5
Damasio, H. 34
Davis, F. 159
death
    commemoration rituals 46*f*, 156–7, 158
    fear of 141
    living wills and preparation for 89, 151
    palliative care and preparation for 145
    songs about 139
    see also funerals; grief
Declaration of the Rights of a Child
    (United Nations) 93
decorations 49
de Haan, T. 30
designing rituals. *see* ritualmaking
disabled participants 99–100, 111, 125
disconnection 33–4
disorientation 28
Dissanayake, E.
    affecting presence 58
    attunement through mother-
        child interactions 23
    emotional quality of rituals 35
    purpose and character of rituals 22, 23, 24
    ritual benefits 153
    ritual content 56
Distanced identities 28*f*, 29–30, 30n5, 75, 90
divorce 135
Douglas, Mary 25
Dutch rituals 46*f*, 156

Eco, U. 64
Economist, The 133
EFT (Emotional Freedom Techniques) 35n6
EMDR (Eye Movement Desensitization
    and Reprocessing) 35n6
emotions and feelings
    reader guidelines for 87
    ritual-derived benefits of 35
    ritualization effects on 37–8, 38, 45, 47
    ritual planning phase and prioritizing 73
    studies on purpose of 34
    see also safe feelings
end of mothering rituals 111–12

environmental issues 48, 49, 125
eulogies (homages) 79, 142, 144, 145, 147–8
expectations 61, 73, 140
Eye Movement Desensitization and
    Reprocessing (EMDR) 35n6

fear 35–6, 38–9n8, 69, 141
Fields, J. 132
France 118n1, 140n1, 151n2, 155
functionalism 51n1, 59
funerals
    and burials 144, 148–9
    emotional expression benefits 38
    examples of 142–5
    function and significance of 139–40, 141
    homages and tributes 147–8
    keepsakes given at 144
    living wills and preparations for 89, 151
    modern practice statistics 26f, 140
    non-religious options and authenticity
        expectations 140
    planning and implementation 138c, 145–9
    prioritizing examples 74
    receptions after 142–3, 144
    risk factors and challenges of
        17–18, 140–1, 150–1
    role attribution and diagrams
        for 55–6, 55f, 142f
    sensemaking examples 79, 83, 84, 85

Gairin, V.140
Gautier, Théophile 58n2
Gawande, Atul 64–5, 66
gestures 84–5, 121
ghost bikes 157
Giraffe Dance 22–3
God (gods) 33
Golden Rule, The 37, 58
Goodman, T. 159
Gordon, Wendy 158
graduation ceremonies 79, 114, 154
Grand, D. 70–1
Great Britain 140, 140n1
greeters 87
grief
    as funeral function 139–41, 149
    ritualization and process of 17–18, 38, 151
    supportive strategies for 150
Grimes, R.L. 51–2, 107, 153
group ritualization 35, 56, 62, 153, 155n4
growing up celebrations 130c, 134
    see also coming of age events
guest books 85, 96, 99

Hall, D.L. 19, 19n1, 163
happiness 131–2
healing
    African tribal rituals for 22–3, 22n1
    funeral ceremonies as 18

trauma resolution techniques and
    ritualization for 35–7, 36f, 38n7
heavenly drum (exercise) 72
Hegel, Georg Wilhelm Friedrich 25n4
Heinskou, M.B. 37, 163
Hermagoras of Temnos 60
Hiroshima bombing 158
Holloway, M. 37, 56, 140
homages (eulogies) 79, 142, 144, 145, 147–8
house destruction rituals 156
hugging 69–70
humanism 25
humming 71
hunter-gatherer societies 22–3, 30, 42, 52, 108

identity 23–4, 28, 36f, 56, 108
    see also ritual identity
IEP (Internet Encyclopedia of Philosophy) 31
Illich, Ivan 63–4
IMC Research 140n1
improvisation 58, 60, 61, 66, 112
indigenous people
    cultural appropriation and
        exploitation of 43–4, 115
    hunter-gatherer traditions 22–3, 30, 42, 52, 108
    public space installations
        commemorating 156–7
individualism 26
Institutional identities 28f, 29, 30n5, 75, 90
Internet Encyclopedia of Philosophy (IEP) 31
interreligious rituals 16, 98–9, 119–20, 121–2
Ireland 118n1

Jarero, I. 70
Jewish exile commemorations 159, 160f
Jewish traditions 98, 99
Jonte-Pace, D. 24

Katz, R. 22–3, 22n1
Kline, T.C., III 37
Könemann, J. 29
Kuhn, T. 16n1
!Kung 22–3

Lacombe, Uma 71
Lakota 44, 115
Lenoir, F. 33
Leonard, A.157–8
Levine, P.A. 33–4, 35, 37, 38, 38n7
Liebst, L.S. 37, 163
'Lighting the spiritual flame' (ritual) 121
living wills 89, 151
Lodoli, Carlo 51n1

Mariani, M. 154n2
marriage 117–18, 135, 136
    see also weddings
materials 28, 50–1, 53, 59
meaningfulness

benefits of 28, 38
design rules for 57–8
requirements for 163
ritual identity and practice challenges in 29–30
trauma resolution and benefits of 37
menopause celebrations 79, 83, 84, 85
menstruation 134
Mies van der Rohe, L. 50–1
military enlistment, as coming
    of age event 110–11
ming of *t'ien* 131
modern culture 33–4
Morely, P.154
music 58, 83–4, 87, 148
Myerhoff, B.62

Nagasaki bombing 158
Names and Numbers 159, 160*f*
naming (new arrival, welcoming) ceremonies
core value expression examples 79
examples of 95–101
function and significance of 94
gestures and symbols examples 84, 94
main ingredients of 95
music selection examples 83
needs assessments for 93
planning and implementation 92*c,* 102–4
risk factors 105
role diagrams for 95*f*
National Funeral Directors
    Association's Report 140n1
near and far (exercise) 70–1
needs 28*f,* 29–30, 36*f,* 54, 58
Neiman, S. 131–2
neurology
creativity requirements 132n2
exercises impacting brain function 71
ritual benefits and brain function 35n6, 38–9n8
stress responses 47
trauma responses 35
new arrival ceremonies. *see* naming ceremonies
New Zealand 118n1
Nietzsche, Friedrich 58–9n2
North America 30n5
Norway 108
Nuit Debout (social movement) 155
num (!Kung energy) 22n1

Occupy Wall Street 154–5
Odate, T. 64
100 Promises for My Child (Chopra) 101

Panksepp, J. 23n2
paradigm shifts 16
parody 43–4
participation 53
parties *vs.* celebrations 47–8
Passacaglia della vita (song) 139
Peace Lantern Ceremony 158

peacemaking circles 158–9
pendulation 38, 38n7
people (participants)
central 55–6, 55*f,* 74, 76*t,* 78–9
disabled 99–100, 111, 125
participation requirements of 53
presiders 55–6, 55*f,* 74–6, 76*t,* 87–8
respect for, as ritual design rule 58
ritual design and role identification 55–6, 55*f*
as ritual material 53
see also craftspeople
People's Path, The 44
Picucci, M. 22
PIPs (Positive Impact Points) 158
place and space
as context variable 54
as ritual material 53
venue selection 48, 54, 86–7, 102–3, 125
weather risks 61
see also public space rituals
Plato 42
playfulness 47, 154
Polyvagal Theory, The (Porges) 37, 38–9n8
Porges, S.W. 36–7, 38–9n8, 132
Positive Impact Points (PIPs) 158
pottery analogies 32
presiders
event responsibilities of 87–8
professional celebrants as 75–6, 76*t*
purpose of 74–5
role descriptions and assignment
    of 55–6, 55*f,* 76*t*
prioritizing exercises 72–4, 73*f*
psychotherapy 45, 163
public space rituals
definition 154n1
examples of 156–9, 160*f*
function and significance 154–5
planning and implementation 152*c,* 156*f,* 160
risk factors 161

readers 88–9, 128
regeneration exercises 71
relationships
authentic ritualization enhancing 36*f*
emotional attunement for bonding 23–4
enhancement of, as ritual pattern
    component 36*f*
respect for, as ritual design rule 58
see also roles
religion
ritual associated with 25–6
ritual identity profiles and attachment to 29–30
unaffiliated population statistics 26*f,* 27, 30n5
unaffiliated ritual identities 90
respect 58
retirement 79, 83, 84, 85, 136
Rites de Passage, Les (van Gennep) 107n1
rites of passage 107–8

see also coming of age events
ritual identity
 as context variable 54
 non-religious celebrants and changes in 18
 professional celebrant hiring and 75
 profile types 29, 90
 questionnaires determining 66–8, 90
 ritual practice selection and 28*f,* 29–30
ritualization, overview
 ancient and historical traditions of 22–3, 31–3
 benefits of 24, 28, 28*f,* 37–9, 62, 163–4
 character descriptions of 19, 30, 43–9
 concept development and evolution of 25–7
 conditions for effective 36*f*
 contexts for 27*f*
 function of 23–4, 26, 30, 33–4
 modern trends in 16, 26–7
 patterns of 36*f*
 requirements for 163
 ritual identity and practice selection 28*f,* 29–30
 sensemaking of 31–3
 terminology origins 19n2
 time and recognition of 24
 see also related topics
ritualmaking
 creative process and phases for 51–2, 51*f,* 60–2
 definition and description 34n4
 design pillars of 53–7
 design rules for 57–60
 guidelines for 43–9
 historical evolution of 42–3
 materials for 28, 50–1, 53, 59
 requirements for 43
 see also tools for ritualmaking
rock art 22
rocking 69
Rock that Whispers 22
roles
 of central people as presiders 74, 76*t*
 as context variable 54
 cooperation and teamwork requirements 47
 identification and assignment of 55–6, 55*f*
 of presiders 74–6, 76*t*
 risk factors associated with 61

safe feelings
 as condition for trauma resolution
  and ritual effectiveness 36*f*
 as creativity requirement 36, 132
 exercises for 68–72
 for healing 35
 importance of 36–7
 as ritual purpose and benefit
  33–4, 38–9, 38–9n8
Sand, David 158
Sand, George 58–9n2
San people 22–3, 42
Sassen, S. 154n2, 155

Scaer, R.C. 23n3, 35–6, 35n6
Schirch, L. 44–5
Schnarch, D.M. 69
Scotland 118
Secular identities 28*f,* 29, 30, 30n5, 90
secularism 16, 25
Seligman, A.B. 19
Senghor, Leopold 58–9n2
sensemaking
 coherence tests determining 82, 83*t*
 Confucian philosophy on 31–3
 core values identification and
  expression for 78–80, 80–1*t*
 creating phase brainstorming for 77
 definition and description 34n3
 funeral planning for 141
 gestures for 84–5
 music selection for 83–4
 as ritual design component 56–7
 as ritual pattern component 36*f*
 signs and symbols for 56, 57, 58, 84–5, 94, 129
Serra, A. 123n2
Shinto traditions 122
Shiru, Deng 32*f*
signs and symbols
 as context variable 52, 54
 for meaningfulness 56, 57, 58, 84–5, 94, 129
simplicity 59–60, 61, 126
Smyth, M. 18, 37, 42, 108, 153
social bonding 23–4, 35, 36*f,* 58, 62
 see also attunement; belonging
social gatherings
 celebrations *vs.* parties 47–8
 for coming of age events 109–10, 110
 for divorce negotiation rituals 135
 for end of mothering rituals 111–12
 funeral receptions 144
 as grief support 150
 memories shared at funerals 143, 144
 with naming ceremonies 94, 100, 102
 risk factors of 62
 for stepfamily cohesion 135
 symbolism of 47, 84
 transition from ceremony to 88
 wedding receptions 49, 118, 120, 125–6
society 23–4, 26, 33–4, 35
Solà-Morales, Ignasi de 154n2
South Africa 118n1, 159
Steinem, G. 61
stepfamily coherence rituals 135
Stolz, J.29
Story of Stuff, The 157–8
stress 33, 47, 69–71
Sung, W. 34, 163
SunLife 140
Sutherland, S.28
Switzerland 29–30, 117, 118n1, 132, 155

tableware 49
Taoism 72
tapping techniques 35n6, 69–70, 72
Tavor, O. 31, 33, 34, 36
teamwork 47
terrain vague 154
TFT (Thought Field Therapy) 35n6
theatricality 46
therapeutic experiences
   as ritual benefit 35, 38–9n8, 45, 163
   trauma resolution 35–6, 36*f*,
      38–9n8, 38n7, 155n4
Thompson, N. 155
time
   ceremony preparation 87
   cognitive timekeeping and stress effects 47
   as context variable 28, 53, 54
   as funeral planning challenge 17–18
   ritualization impact on 24, 47
   trauma resolution rituals impact on 35–6, 36*f*
   truth to materials and right 28, 59
Tomatis, A. 23n2, 71, 72
tools for ritualmaking
   ceremony format planning 85–7
   checklists as 64–6
   coherence tests 82, 83*t*
   core values identification and
      expression 78–80, 80–1*t*
   funeral preparation 89
   gestures and symbols 84–5
   mapping it out 81–2
   music selection 83–4
   presider selection and role
      descriptions 74–6, 76*t*
   prioritizing exercises 72–4, 73*f*
   reader guidelines 88–9
   requirements of 63–4
   ritual identity questionnaires 66–8, 90
   ritual purpose brainstorming exercises 77
   safe feeling exercises 68–72
Traditional identities 90
trauma
   of death 141
   effects of 33–4, 35
   public space rituals for apartheid 159
   ritualizing for resolution of 35–6,
      36*f*, 38–9n8, 38n7, 155n4
travel 48, 110, 125, 134
tributes 148
TRIPODS (Titrating, Resourcing, Integrating,
   Pendulating, Organizing, Discharging,
   Stabilizing) process 38n7
troubleshooting 87

Truth and Reconciliation Commission (TRC) 159
truthfulness 61
truth to materials 28, 51n1, 59

Ueland, B. 60
Ukraine 132
Unaffiliated identities 26*f*, 27, 30n5, 90
United Kingdom 118n1
United States 118, 118n1, 140n1

vagal nerve exercises 71
values, core 78–80, 80–1*t*, 82, 83*t*
van der Kolk, B.A. 23n3, 35, 38–9n8, 47n1
van der Lee, Ida 159, 160*f*
van Dillen, Imke 156
van Gelder, S. 132
van Gennep, A. 107n1
venues 48, 54, 86–7, 102–3, 125
visual convergence exercises 70–1

Walking with Our Sisters (installation) 156–7
waste reduction 48
Watford, Destiny 158
Watson, B. 31n1
weather 61
weddings
   core value expression examples 79
   environmentally-conscious options 49
   examples of 119–24
   function and significance of 117–18
   gestures and symbols examples 84, 85
   in history 117
   music selection examples 83
   options for 118–19
   order of, sample 128
   personalization of unconventional 16–17
   planning and implementation 116*c*, 124–8
   prioritizing exercise example for 74
   receptions after 49, 118, 120, 125–6
   risk factors 129
   role descriptions and diagrams for 56, 119*f*
   same-sex 118, 121
   vows for 117, 120, 121, 122, 123, 125–7, 127*f*
welcoming ceremonies. *see* naming ceremonies
wills, living 89, 151
wisdom, seven basic rules of 123
Wojtkowiak, J. 148
World War II commemorative
   rituals 158, 159, 160*f*

Xunzi 31–3, 31n1, 32*f*, 34, 36, 37, 45

Zoroastrian traditions 121

Jeltje Gordon-Lennox is an author and psychotherapist with expertise in the field of world religions, writing about ritual studies theory and the role of the senses in the contemporary practice of secular ritual. She is the founder of the Ashoka Association (Ashoka.ch), where she trains secular celebrants in the craft of secular ritualization. Jeltje lives in Switzerland.